Praise for *Over It*

"In a world that sends an 'unspoken message of perfection' Kelsey's sweet spirit and willingness to share her vulnerable story of shame and self-discovery is a breath of fresh air. I'll take an authentic read of personal experience, hard work, and triumph any day of the week!"

—**Heather Land,** comedian, author, and recording artist

"To me, this is more than a book. It's words out of my own mouth! Even with our differences, we feel the same systematic pressure. I cried and laughed all in the same chapter. The message of this book is a must-hear!"

—**Cara Clark,** nutritionist, author, and TV personality

"I'm a fan! Anyone brave enough to get this honest and real is a force to be reckoned with. For all of us who need a shot of courage, truth, and grace—this book is a must. Well done, Kelsey!"

—**Grace Valentine,** author, podcast host, and speaker

"It takes courage and kindness to look back on the things that broke us. Kelsey's story is a reminder that every fragment of our life matters and can be reconciled."

—**Moriah Smallbone,** recording artist, producer, and podcast creator

"I relate to this message on such a deep level. In this book, Kelsey breaks loose the shackles of expectations that many of us women carry every day. We have been taught to prove ourselves and strive for acceptance. But along with Kelsey, I'm OVER IT."

—**Madison Prewett,** author, speaker, and TV personality

OVER IT

Forgetting Who You're Expected to Be
and Becoming Who You Already Are

KELSEY GRIMM

New York • Nashville

Worthy Publishing
Hachette Book Group
1290 Avenue of the Americas, New York, NY 10104
worthypublishing.com
twitter.com/worthy

First Edition: September 2021

Worthy is a division of Hachette Book Group, Inc.
The Worthy name and logo are trademarks of Hachette Book Group, Inc.

The publisher is not responsible for websites (or their content) that are not owned by the publisher.

The Hachette Speakers Bureau provides a wide range of authors for speaking events. To find out more, go to www.hachettespeakersbureau.com or call (866) 376-6591.

LCCN: 2021939219

ISBNs: 978-1-5460-1566-6 (hardcover), 978-1-5460-1565-9 (ebook)

Printed in the United States of America
LSC-C
Printing 1, 2021

To my Caleb. For holding me up and
being my rock every step of the way.
You're the reason I believe in love again.

CONTENTS

OVER IT

Introduction

WHAT'S YOUR "IT"?

Okay, so let's be real, y'all.

And I don't mean "let's share safe surfacy socially acceptable stuff." Like, I'm so over that. And we've all done it. In small group on Wednesday night, or the Zoom Bible study, or even coffee dates with friends. The topics that are like "I just feel like I should be spending more time in my devos." Or "I should really try to be more organized and stay ahead of laundry, so it doesn't consume me." Or this one: "I should really start working out more because these other moms are seemingly finding time for self-care and it's probably important." Or "I'm just a stay-at-home mom, so I should try to pursue something on the side so I feel like I'm contributing more."

Nah, girl. Let me paint the real scene for you: I'm sitting here with no makeup on, greasy hair that hasn't been washed since last Saturday probably because #momlife, and in the same yoga pants I've worn the last four days in a row. But I'm across the couch from you, eye to eye, about to dump all my deepest insecurities and the lies I tell myself every day, a bunch of reasons I'm not enough. See if any of these hit home for you too:

I'm too broken to love again.

I'm too broken to be loved again.

If I tell myself I'm okay, I can be okay.

I can get through hardship on my own.

I don't need other people.

God shouldn't use someone as messed up as I am.

I don't deserve to be used and to see my dreams become
    reality.

Because of my platform, I need to have my life together.
    People are watching.

If I can control my surroundings, I will feel secure.

If I can measure up to what I think people want me to be,
    I'll be fulfilled and happy.

My achievements are what make me influential and
    valuable.

God will only bless me if I'm walking in His way.

I can be who people need (or want) me to be.

What I do makes me who I am.

If my body looked *that* way or I weighed less, I'd feel
    comfortable in my own skin.

My guess is that you probably either resonate with some (or maybe even all) of those things or you're going, *Geez, girl, you got ISSUES* (tell me something I *don't* know).

For real, though, that list? It pretty much sums up the things I've told myself for most of my life. Just rereading it now makes me tired. Like, it's exhausting. And the thing that every freaking line of that fifteen-item list has in common can be boiled down to two words: false expectations. Soul-grinding, depression-inducing expectations I've placed on myself or allowed to be placed on me by the world.

So, no. I'm not a have-it-all-together author standing up here writing to you down there. And really, if I'm being honest, I'm not even qualified to write a book telling other women how to think, live, or feel. So, breathe—because I'm not going to *should* on you. Culture does that to us incessantly. I'm not going to be another echo chamber getting all up in your business telling you what you should do, be, or think. And besides, we do that enough to ourselves every day. Amiright?

Before we dig in, I want to let you know why I decided to write this book in the first place. I honestly felt like it was a culmination of a lot of hard years colliding with the courage to finally share my story in hopes it might help someone else… maybe you. In fact, a couple of years ago, before the idea to write it was ever born, a friend asked me how I would describe my life over the last decade or so in one word. I hardly even had to think about it before I saw the word come to mind in bold letters: *hard*. Don't get me wrong; there have been plenty of incredible mountaintop experiences that I will carry with me for the rest of my life, but so much of the last dozen years resembles a pattern of long, dark seasons strung together by occasional bright ones here or there.

So one of the reasons for writing was for my own health. I needed to get out of my head and heart and get down on paper what I had been through, what I had learned, and where I wanted to go. For me. From there, I started to realize that the more I told my story—the story you are about to read—the more stories I received from people like you who resonate with it. By simply sharing my pain and being as open and vulnerable as possible, I made a connection with other women (mainly) who, like me, desperately wanted out from underneath the suffocating pressure of performance and expectation. Just like the title says, they, like me, were over it.

Over the guilt.

Over the shame.

Over the second-guessing.

Over the self-hatred.

Over the pervasive need to be perfect.

Just. Over. IT!

In some ways, this is more a narrative than it is a "teaching" book. I'm not a therapist, pastor, or counselor. In fact, my hope is that as you read my story, it will be more like sitting under a blanket across from each other on the couch talking over a cup of coffee. Just sharing our stories, our hopes, and our dreams like best friends.

Right up front there's something I need you to know. I was raised in a very loving, tight-knit family. My parents were—and are—incredible people who've truly loved me unconditionally every step of the way and have given me space and freedom to step into my true self. They're still my husband's, Caleb, and my best friends on the planet. And they are phenomenal grandparents to our two boys, Emmett and Beckett, and our daughter, Collins.

But juxtaposed with that, however, was the conservative cultural bubble I was raised in. Evangelical, embedded with a *lot* of silent expectations—like, I was born into this invisible river of expectations. If you were raised in a Christian environment, you will probably relate to some or a lot of my story. Yes, I did learn about a Jesus who is real and loving and whose love for me is unconditional. And at the same time, another subtle but very different message was at play: If you do the right things, say the right things, and act the right way, you will prove yourself to be a "good" Christian and God will not withhold from you His blessings.

Was that message preached from the pulpit? No. Did my parents raise me to believe that? Absolutely not. But the conservative American Christian culture that shaped me most certainly modeled that message. And it had a deep, lingering, and damaging effect on me (as you will see).

But I want to make something crystal clear—this is *not* an ax-grinding, "why the church is terrible" book. Not even a little bit. I have a deep love for the church to this day. But this *is* the story of a girl who came to believe—wrongly—that her worth was measured more by who she was, not *whose* she was. And I was shaped by an unspoken set of rules and standards of conduct and behavior.

So, yes, conservative Christian culture had its flaws and laid some of the groundwork for the expectations I tried to live up to initially. But you want to know what it's grown into? You want to know what else has spoken into the silent expectations us girls are hit with every day in real time? The current culture we're living in now. The curated, Photoshopped, idealistic culture that screams at us and hits us from every angle, everywhere we turn.

The messages are loud and clear. Today's culture tells us exactly what we're supposed to be: what our bodies should look like, where our beauty and worth lie, our level of success based on what we can offer the world, how we should interact with others, and what our relationships with them should look like. It tells us what to eat, what to wear, how to carry ourselves, how to raise our children, what makeup to use, how often we should work out, and what our goals should be.

The world is very clear about these expectations—do everything and look good doing it. Be a perfect career woman, wife, mom, daughter, friend, sister, and so on. Balance it all with grace and ease. Be attractive, but not too sexy. Be confident, but not too loud. Pursue your goals, but also raise perfect kids. Work out and eat right, but be comfortable in your own skin. Don't let anyone take advantage of you, but be accommodating and polite no matter what. Look put-together, but don't be vain.

Like, here's an example of one of my typical "working-day-in-the-life" schedules of this usual stay-at-home mom:

6:00 a.m.: Wake up an hour before the rest of the house. Wash face. Drink coffee in quiet peace.

6:15: Work out.

6:45: Take a shower without a tiny audience asking for a million things (actually wash hair).

7:00: Wake the children, who slept peacefully through the night.

7:30: Make a well-balanced breakfast that everyone eats happily.

8:00: Hair and makeup team arrive to prepare for video shoot while children play independently and quietly on their own.

9:30: Put the littlest baby down for her nap without a fight.

10:00: Kiss the toddler boys and grab clothes for shoot and head out the door on time and prepared for the day.

12:00–4:00 p.m.: Shoot series of music videos that go smoothly.

5:00: Arrive back home to happy children.

5:30: Cook another well-balanced meal that said children eat without arguing, then clean it up.

6:00: Play with children and read books together.

7:00: Bathe children, brush teeth, and sit and talk about the day.

8:00: Pray and kiss children good night. They all fall asleep and need nothing.

9:00: Pour glass of wine and take an Epsom salt bath.

9:30: Have passionate, great sex with husband after a riveting conversation about life and the future with him.

10:00: In bed, lights out, children sleep through the night.

PSYCH! Here's what it actually looks like on days that I'm working (video shoots, recording days, etc.):

6:00 a.m.: The children are awake well before me—screaming on the monitor to come get them up (after I've been up twice already during the night to nurse one who still doesn't sleep through the night).

6:15: Bring all the children to bed with me so I can nurse one while the other two jump on the bed between Caleb and me as we try to squeeze in ten more minutes of dozing.

6:30: Peel myself out of bed and drag my butt to get coffee while all the tiny children make their needs and demands known.

6:45: Deny them candy for the first time in the day (*It's not even 7 a.m. yet, guys!*) and settle for throwing a Lärabar at them so I can drink my coffee in "peace" for three minutes and try to wake up while they watch *Daniel Tiger*.

7:00: Listen to the children make more demands. Say no to candy for the second time.

7:30: Finally convince myself to turn off the TV and make them play and do something that uses their brains.

8:00: Hair and makeup arrives, and I'm still scrambling to find a bra and pants.

8:30: Hair and makeup starts on my *very* tired face, and we get interrupted 3,238,795 times by children needing various things (one needs his butt wiped, one needs a boob, one needs another snack). Say no to candy for third time.

9:30: Baby is fussy since she was up three times the night before. Pause hair and makeup to pacify baby.

10:00: Finish hair and makeup. Scramble to find clothes and shoes and jam them into a bag. I'm already running fifteen minutes behind schedule and should've been out the door at 9:45.

10:15: Grab youngest baby and diaper bag and rush out the door (can't leave baby at home because she's nursing and can't be left with a nanny yet).

11:00–4:00 p.m.: Shoot a series of videos with littlest baby in tow, so we get interrupted eighty-seven times.

4:30: Finally wrap the last video and load up and out. Put baby in car seat for forty-five-minute drive home while she screams because she didn't nap the entire day.

5:15: Finally get home with screaming baby. Unload the car. Come inside to two other crabby toddlers (because 5:00 p.m. is the witching hour) demanding dinner (and, of course, candy).

5:30: Pull out hot dogs and mac and cheese and call it dinner—which no one eats after asking for dinner.

6:00: Everyone is in meltdown mode. Early baths. Children ask for snacks (and candy) for the 22,342nd time that day. Turn on a show for testy kids again while I change into sweats and take bra off again.

7:30: Finally wrestle the children to bed, but walk up the stairs four different times for various other needs and demands (water cup, bathroom light on, dropped a paci, final hail Mary attempt at candy, etc.).

8:30: Collapse on couch. Husband pours me a glass of wine. We try to talk and connect, but I'm falling asleep.

9:00: Peel self off of couch to brush teeth and fall into bed before being awakened at 2:00 a.m. to nurse the baby.

You guys. This is what a work day *actually* looks like for me. It's exhausting, isn't it?

Like, it's not great. I want to be able to do it all and do it all well. I want to be able to work, be a mom and wife, connect with friends, and have time for self-care—but *how*? On most days it's impossible. I wind up falling into bed before 10:30 p.m., utterly exhausted, defeated, and feeling inadequate on all fronts. I just can't live up to all the expectations I feel every day. It's crippling.

Anybody feel me here?

But I'm here to tell you guys I'm learning—and starting to break free from the feeling of being weighed down by it all.

Before we dive in further, I am going to give you a few major spoilers here—but I think it's a good jumping-off point:

Spoiler #1: There *is* an answer to the question *Can I ever break free from the expectations and pressures I'm hit with all the time?* And wait for it—the answer is, *yes*, you can (but not by yourself).

Spoiler #2: The path you take to get over it—whatever *it* is—will probably look a hell of a lot different than you think. (Sorry. But it's true.)

Spoiler #3: You can't do this alone. We were never meant to journey through life alone. So asking for help— whether it's in counseling, or confiding in a friend or mentor—is not weak. It's brave. We need one another.

Spoiler #4: You're already loved. And you're already enough. Just as you sit in this moment right here, reading this. Having dreams and goals of being the best version of yourself is great, but not at the expense of losing your true identity. Your true identity lies in the fact that you're already loved, valuable, and treasured by the One who created you.

Close your eyes and think of your "it" (don't roll your eyes at me, just do it for a minute). The thing you're leaning into that's sucking the life out of you. The expectations you're trying to live up to but you're failing miserably at. Maybe it's what other people think of you. Maybe it's a betrayal. Maybe it's a dark secret you're keeping because you have to look like you've got it together. Maybe it's a broken relationship. A crippling death. A diagnosis of disease. A lost dream. An addiction. A body image issue. Maybe it's a past regret that keeps you up at night. If you're anything like me, it might be several "its" strung together…I mean, you read my list. But they eat at you. Take up space and energy in your heart and mind. You can't shake them. You can't seem to break free of them.

Because the truth is: We're human. We're multifaceted. We're messy, and most of us have lots of issues—very rarely is it just one. So, I'm here for it. Hit me with your list. I promise you'll get the full story of mine and the consequences of them the more you read on.

One more thing before we start: Even if your list is enormous—as in, a Mount Freaking Everest of pain and heartbreak and darkness within you—there is hope, I *promise.* Trust me, I've been the girl who wanted to throw it all away once.

So make a deal with me. Will you open your heart up to at least the *possibility* of hope for where you're at right now? Will you open yourself up to the idea that you're already loved? That you're already enough? That you don't have to keep living under the paralyzing standards culture and society rub in our faces every day? That there's a better way of living, learning, and loving if we only open our eyes and see our inherent worth?

More than anything, I want to thank you and encourage you. Thank you for trusting me enough to go on this journey with me. I'm just a little ol' transplanted Midwestern girl telling her story—but in some ways, it represents *all* of our stories. And, yeah, I do want to encourage you. Even if you've been abandoned by everyone who's ever loved you or whom you've ever loved. Because even then, you're *not* alone. You're *already* loved, and nothing you do can change that.

So cheers to this wild ride we're about to go on together.

Chapter 1

ONCE UPON A DARK AND STORMY NIGHT

Would it be too clichéd to start off by saying that it happened on a dark and stormy night?

I mean, isn't that how clichés become clichés? Because some universal truth echoes through them?

Well, it was. Very dark and very stormy. In every way.

My life was a disaster. Like, a natural disaster. There I was, twenty-three years old, living in a beautiful home in Nashville, dating attractive guys, being invited to freaking awesome parties—all while living out my dream of being a professional recording artist. I had *finally* made it. It's what I had wanted my entire life.

Only, that dream had turned out to be a nightmare.

Growing up, what I absorbed in my spiritual journey was that if you prayed hard enough for something, and you behaved well enough to deserve it, God would give it to you because you'd worked hard to stay in His will for you. But that wasn't my story as I drove through the rain. Because me? I felt nothing. Nothing and everything at the same time. I was hollow, and it hurt like hell.

A normal person would probably do some introspection. Change up their lifestyle. Some counseling, maybe. But me?

Enter Hurricane Kelsey.

She had a lot of movement, plenty of destruction, and very little direction or predictability.

When I'm feeling especially anxious or antsy, sometimes I find myself running from it all. This particular night my escape plan was to take a long, dark drive alone. So on that stormy night in 2012, that's what I did. And even though I wanted to be pissed off and indignant, I was actually terrified. Filled to the brim with shame. I hated the person I had become.

I'll never forget how hard it was raining. I don't know if I recall it ever raining that hard since. The kind of rain that slaps across your windshield in sheets so violently that you'd swear the glass was going to shatter. That's all I heard as I drove in silence with nowhere to go and no one on my side anymore.

The backroads of Nashville were empty. I liked it that way. So I drove around aimlessly, scared to death about what would happen next. Because I knew I had messed up *for real* this time. And I was pretty sure there was nothing I could do to fix it.

The *it* I was failing to fix was me—my entire life, really. I'd just recently graduated from college. I'd broken off a really unhealthy engagement to my fiancé, Chris (not his real name), and I was trying to put back together the pieces of my shattered life. I had nowhere to go and no bright future ahead of me. I spent that entire summer hopping from one metaphorically numbing drug to another. It was a summer of meaningless relationships, late-night bad decisions, and dishonesty.

My parents were terrified for me. They tried tirelessly to talk to me, to open the lines of communication and figure out why I was spiraling out of control.

But I kept to myself. They could never know about what Chris did to me. What I *allowed* Chris to do to me. At the tail end of that tumultuous summer, I was offered an opportunity to audition for a new Christian girl pop group in Nashville, and since I had nothing to lose, I decided to go for it. After making the group, I had moved to Music City to embark on becoming the Spice Girls of the Christian world.

I had such high hopes of erasing my past and starting over in Nashville, where no one knew me. I wanted to forget the pain I'd stuffed deep down for all those months. But it turns out, you can't outrun your pain. It catches up with you, and it had followed me straight to Nashville. I didn't get the fresh start that I was so desperate for.

In fact, my bad decisions picked up right where they left off, just in a new city. I partied. I went out. I drank. In fact, I was coming off another long weekend of binge-drinking and irresponsible sexual decisions.

It had been almost a year since my abusive fiancé and I had split, but I still drank on it. And drank some more. I medicated it with any distraction I could get my hands on.

Because I didn't know what else to do with the pain. And here I was again—in another unhealthy relationship that I knew was bad for me and headed for nowhere.

The roads I drove down were narrow and winding. Usually, I'd find comfort in that—in the beauty and peacefulness of the rain splashing on empty fields in the middle of nowhere. But not tonight. Every twist reminded me of the things I didn't see coming. That no matter where I went or how far I tried to run, there would always be turns that I could never anticipate. I was afraid of the darkness that I knew lived inside me and felt it would never go away.

If you've ever been in an abusive or toxic relationship, you know the labels that come with them: *Unworthy. Unlovable. Irredeemable.* But you need to know up front that my reason for writing is not to tell you about that toxic relationship. Sure, that's part of my story. But the main goal in sharing my story is to tell you what led me down the road to that relationship—and what led me out. Mostly, it was expectations inside my head that were either flat-out wrong or very, very skewed. Expectations about myself—who I thought others wanted me to be, and who I thought I needed to be.

As I drove that night, it felt like I had made it in the Christian music scene—but that still wasn't enough, because I would never be enough.

I wasn't well. The people around me knew it, I knew it, and I was too ashamed to go to God with it.

Earlier that day my manager had called me in. He was like, "Look. You have to get a handle on this, Kelsey. I don't know what else to do. I can't keep you on board if you keep acting out.

I'm trying to help you. I need you to listen to me; I need you to listen to *somebody*."

I think I mumbled something that resembled an apology, but we all knew I wasn't changing anything. Then I took off in my car—and a dark afternoon turned into an even darker night.

Somehow, over the sound of the downpour, I heard the faint buzz of my cell phone. I fumbled to grab it and look at the caller ID: DADDY

Here's the thing you need to know about my dad—he doesn't get mad. Almost ever. I can count on one hand the number of times he has ever been so angry that he raised his voice at me. Add this night to the one hand.

I don't even think I had even said hello before he started laying into me.

"Kelsey! What are you doing?! Are you trying to ruin your life? Did we not raise you to be better than this? What is your problem?! You better get yourself straightened out or you will lose everything. This is insane. Your manager is terrified, your mother is terrified, I'm terrified. Get it together."

Then he hung up.

I dropped my phone and stared straight ahead, squinting. Because now I was battling the rain *and* my tears.

Kelsey, your dad just screamed at you. Now you've lost everyone. Good. Freaking. Job. Slow clap for your stellar character and judgment.

But honestly, I knew he was right. He was justified. He wasn't demeaning—he was scared. And I got it, because I was scared, too.

Tears turned to sobs. Like, that real ugly cry where no sound comes out at first and then all of a sudden, it's a tidal wave overtaking you. It's so strong, you can't catch your breath. I gripped the steering wheel until my knuckles turned white.

You know how some people have a rock bottom? Well, my rock bottom apparently has a trap door. And I had just fallen through it to somewhere so full of despair that I knew I'd never be okay again.

I've never been a suicidal person, but it crossed my mind in that moment. Steering wheel still in hand, the idea entered my mind.

Just veer off the road, Kelsey. Just drive straight into a tree, off a bridge, anything to end this sorry excuse for a life.

Then my phone buzzed again. This time I had to reach beneath the driver's seat to get to it. I glanced at the screen: DADDY.

I didn't know if I should answer. I couldn't take any more. I really thought about letting it go to voicemail, but I didn't.

"Baby." My dad's voice broke. "I'm sorry. Please forgive me. We just want you to feel whole again. Please, let me help you. Talk to me. Just let me be your daddy, baby. Help me *help you*."

Have you ever had a movie moment in your life? There's a surreal quality to it. A moment that happens where it almost feels like you're watching it from outside your body? That second phone call from my dad was a movie moment. It changed the trajectory of my life indefinitely.

For as long as I could remember, I had been living a life that was driven by what I thought other people wanted from me. I was trying to be…

Who I felt like my parents wanted me to be.

Who the men in my life wanted me to be.

Who my church wanted me to be.

Who my friends wanted me to be.

Even who *I* wanted me to be.

I was failing, and it was literally killing me.

I know we don't know each other personally, but I can say that I'm probably not the only person who has ever felt suffocated by the absurdity of expectations. Expectations took me places that Jesus never called me to. They led me into broken relationships, bad business deals, and bars.

My vain efforts to be everything to everyone brought me around people who weren't interested in who I was but in what I did. Not how I could be friends *with* them, but how I could be an advantage *for* them.

Maybe you're like me and you're *over it*. You're ready to *live* your *own* life. To *own* your *own* life. A life that is free from trying to be an Instagram model or a Pinterest mom or a perfect preacher's wife.

Trying to keep up with expectations is exhausting. It's as exhausting and useless as trying to hide from God—you can't do it. I don't know where you're at in life as you read this book, but I do know that in any and every season, expectations meet us there. Haunting us and taunting us—relentless in stealing our joy and our identity.

I'm a work in process, for sure. I am *not* writing from a place

> Expectations took me places that Jesus never called me to.

of arrival or all-put-togetherness. That's important to know. I am also not a trained psychologist—there are many excellent books out there that provide professional advice on overcoming the issues I've struggled with: low self-esteem, shame, self-guilt, and people pleasing.

I'm writing because if my story can help you see, even in a small way, that your default position with God isn't less, it's *more*, then it's all worth it. He accepts you and loves you more than you can imagine. Another cliché? Yeah, probably. But no less true. You are a pearl of great price, but maybe you don't feel like it. I know I didn't, particularly on that stormy night on the back roads of Nashville. My pearl had been through the mud— tarnished, abused, and tossed around.

> Your default position with God isn't less, it's *more*.

My hope is that by the end of my story, you'll be over the expectations. That you'll be able to live confidently, love selflessly, and experience freedom like you've only ever dreamed of.

Chapter 2

THE HALLWAY

People have all kinds of responses to the things I do—especially on social media. Like when my youngest, Collins, was tiny, I'd put her in this dreamy little swing that gently swayed from side to side. Cut to: All the mothers on Instagram who have somehow managed to *never* put down their newborns, telling me that I'm ensuring Collins's foray into future deviance by not attaching her to my person twenty-four hours a day. My DMs were smokin' hot that day—and not in a good way.

As I've grown older and more confident in who God created me to be, I am less apologetic about the choices I make. But I won't lie—I cried into a glass of wine that night. Mostly, I was pissed, but I was also hurt that someone would think I don't love and treasure Collins with every molecule of my being. Because I do. Oh my Lord, I *do*.

I think that's it—the fear of others' reactions has held me back from telling many people the full story of my life of false expectations. Do you ever wonder what you would do if you weren't afraid? My answer to that question—of facing one of my greatest fears—is writing this book. It's telling you about the moments in my life that have caused me the greatest pain and the greatest shame. Why? Well, that's a more complicated answer.

My reason for writing is to share my journey to overcome false, toxic, and debilitating expectations that nearly crippled and killed me. You know the story of the frog in the kettle? So you put a frog in a cool pot of water and slowly turn up the heat. You know what will happen? The frog will stay right there; it will literally boil to death. Why? Because the temperature changes so slowly that by the time the frog even realizes it's in danger, it's too late. (This is morbid, I know.)

I'm not super psyched at the idea of comparing myself to a frog, but it's a pretty good analogy of what my life was like leading up to that dark night a decade ago—the night I almost drove my car off a bridge. And, yeah, my fall into darkness really gained momentum when I met Chris. But the water in my emotional and spiritual pot was already near boiling by that time.

Another way to look at it is that I was like a disintegrating star and Chris was the black hole that I was hurtling toward. I'd been disintegrating for some time, and it was inevitable that I would destruct. My relationship with Chris just happened to be a pathway toward my implosion.

I want to take a moment to say something here. If you saw the cover of this book and picked it up thinking it would be a lighthearted glimpse into the life of a girl weighed down by life's expectations, I want you to know this story goes deeper than the surface level. So a little disclaimer: If you're hoping to get a feel-good story on breaking free of those expectations, this book may not be for you. And that's okay. Because the truth is that this story is messy, it's dark, and it's full of twists and turns.

Ultimately, it's the story of a girl whose need to live up to others' standards literally almost killed her. (And hi, I am that girl.) So read on, but know that it gets really ugly before the light shines again. I also want to be clear about something else—this is *not* a #MeToo book. There's an element of that in my story. But it's not what this book and the message are about. It's so much more.

So here we are. Here's the story of a girl who learned how to let go.

IIIIIIIIIIIIIIIIIIIIIIIIII

I didn't wake up one day and casually find myself being abused by the man I loved. I decided myself there. I behaved myself there. I grew to there. Does that make sense? Every part of my life up until that point prepared (or underprepared) my heart, my mind, and my spirit to become a victim and future survivor of sexual and emotional abuse.

Before we get to the abuse, I have to start at the beginning. And I have a feeling a lot of you can relate to the story I am about to tell, whether you've been in an abusive relationship or not.

I grew up in a conservative Christian home—I was a pastor's kid, in fact. And probably just like every other pastor's kid on the planet, I always felt this invisible pressure to have it all together. Pressure to follow the (mostly silent) rules.

Rule #1: You don't have to be *perfect*, but if you make a mess, clean it up ASAP. No one likes a mess, and people are watching.

Rule #2: Know all the answers. Know what you believe in stone. If you don't, you'll be easily swayed and pushed into darkness.

Rule #3: Be *in* the world, not *of* it. Like, love people but also don't be around the wrong ones.

I'm most certain that it was never the intention of the role models and voices that shaped me to explicitly force on me this unspoken message of perfection. And I'm also open to the possibility that I could've misinterpreted parts of it along the way. But the fact is, what I absorbed was that at all costs, the most important thing was keeping my life on the up-and-up. To be "above reproach."

I want to pause and make an important distinction here that will set the tone for the rest of the book: My obsessive desire to be "above reproach" slowly turned into making sure I simply *appeared* "above reproach," which became the breeding ground for dishonesty and secrets. Why? Because for me, living above reproach was an impossible feat—but *not* living above reproach was not an option. A classic lose–lose situation, right? So instead of admitting that I could not do it (admitting I was, you know, *human*), I pretended that I could. Predictably, like all of us, I tried and failed.

Even though the ones who loved me would have helped me, I *thought* I was alone. I (wrongly) believed that if I admitted I was not above reproach, well, that would not be acceptable. That's how shame took over my life: These messages (mostly unspoken) of always needing to look okay set me up for the toxic relationship I was about to plunge into. Yes, I made those choices and am responsible for them. I stood on that cliff and willingly took the jump. But there were a lot of false messages and beliefs in my head that influenced my decision to take the dive.

This book is not about the relationship—it's about the inner world of perfectionism I lived in (and have battled to escape from) that made me an ideal candidate for disaster.

So instead of being given the permission to not be okay or put-together all the time, I simply kept the outward appearance in check, while the inside of me began a downward spiral because it couldn't keep up. I just didn't feel like there was a whole lot of room to be a mess.

Looking back, I can only remember a few times when I actually deviated from the rules. It was *so* important to me to be *good*. And based on much of what I was hearing at church and seeing around me, being good meant never getting in trouble. It meant never being the problem—never *having* a problem.

Again, this was my *perception*—in recent years as I've grown healthier and worked through a lot of my perfectionism, I've learned that these things were never the expectation of me in reality. Basically what I'm getting at here is that no one ever told me explicitly that I had to have it all together—but I inferred it through the actions and attitudes of the people who influenced me.

I can count on one hand the number of times I got in trouble growing up, because I was programmed to behave, to not make too much noise, or to never push (or even tap) the envelope.

The first time was when I was in kindergarten. And I did it on purpose.

I started noticing that every time a kid got into trouble in class, the teacher would send them into the hallway. And this is such an indicator of my future personality, but I *had* to know what was going on in that hallway. *The hallway.* A mystical place. What were these kids experiencing in the hallway that I wasn't? Was it cool out there? Did fifth graders walk by and say hi?

Was there a party in the hallway that I was missing out on?

So, I made a choice. Circle time came, and I knew it was the perfect opportunity to put my plan into action. As soon as the teacher opened the read-aloud book, I started acting out. I rolled around on the carpet. I whispered in people's ears. I mean, who even knows what I was saying? Probably just making wispy noises and being annoying. But it did the trick.

"Kelsey?" my teacher said, closing the book and looking at me with blatant shock. I *never* misbehaved. Never. And then, "Let's go into the hallway."

I was the master of the universe in that moment. I was finally going to see what happened out in the great, wild yonder of *the hallway.* I was completely giddy.

My teacher told me to sit with my back against the wall until she came back to get me. So I sat, just waiting for the magic to happen. And I waited. And I waited. And I waited.

Guess what? No, really. Just guess.

Nothing happened in the hallway. Literally nothing. Not a living soul passed by. And it smelled like dirty gym socks and pine-scented Lysol. I rocked back against the scratchy cement wall. *Perhaps I miscalculated the level of fun being had in THE HALLWAY.*

Then my FOMO (fear of missing out) went the other direction. *What are they doing in the classroom? Circle time is taking longer than I remember. Are they having a great time? Are they getting treats? Why did I do this?* Then, *Mom and Dad are gonna be so mad at me.*

I was right. When I got home, my parents had already heard about the scandalous circle time incident, and I got in trouble there as well. My maiden voyage into deviance was underwhelming, to say the least.

It took me literally five more years before I was brave enough to break another rule.

If you met me now, you'd never guess it, but I had some definite tomboy in my DNA growing up. We lived out in the country in Michigan. My younger brothers, Tyler and Chad, and I would meet up with some of the other kids who lived nearby, and we'd run around the fields and yards acting wild. Playing in the dirt and mud. Catching animals to play with.

I remember this one summer I was obsessed with snakes. No, you read that right. I said snakes. In particular, I loved garter snakes. I thought they were adorable. I wanted one as a pet. Want to know my mom's biggest fear in the whole entire universe?

Garter snakes.

So this one day, we're out playing and I catch the cutest little snake baby you've ever seen. My mom had made it abundantly clear that we were *not* to bring critters in the house. Chiefly, snakes.

I get into the house and cup my precious snake angel against my chest and race past my mom through the hallway and into my bedroom. I had this toy bassinette, and I just *knew* my adorable snake baby would look so sweet tucked under a blanket inside of it. But before I could get him there, I tossed him on my bed to get a better look at him.

"Kelsey!" my mom called down the hallway. "What do you have in there?" (By the way, as a mom myself now, I totally get the whole moms-have-a-sixth-sense-and-see-everything thing. My mom knew I was up to something.)

I didn't answer. I was enthralled. When my mom tells the story, she says that when she opened my bedroom door, I was on my knees beside my bed, stroking the snake and talking to it as if it were a newborn. (And don't worry, I'm afraid of snakes now as an adult; I'm not a total psychopath.)

Cue: A monumentally (totally warranted) hysterical fit pitched by my mother.

Needless to say, it was high school before I was brave enough to cross another line.

So let me just say something here. It's not *bad* to want to behave. It's not *bad* to want to be good. It's not even *bad* to respect the traditions of your faith or your parents' faith. But when being "good" becomes the expectation—when it becomes your *identity*—you can expect disappointment. You can expect shame. You can expect self-loathing. Because perfection was never expected of us. Perfection was meant for Jesus. And only Jesus.

But for me, the message was clear. Good girls don't break the rules. Grace? Forgiveness? Mercy? (You know, the entire purpose of Jesus' life and death?) These concepts were overshadowed by the "be good, do good" culture of my formative years. If you messed up, you needed to get right back on track as fast as possible and move forward.

> When being "good" becomes the expectation—when it becomes your *identity*—you can expect disappointment.

In some ways, I grew up in a box. A porcelain doll. *Hiiiiigh* up on a shelf. Every award, every accolade, every solo I sang at church, every A I made in school, *everything* I did that made me feel *good* surrounded me on that shelf. Glass artifacts of a girl living to please everyone, everywhere.

And when the weight of reality pressed down on that shelf, everything came crashing down—me included—shattering to the floor into a thousand tiny pieces.

Chapter 3

SIT DOWN, SHUT UP, AND PLAY NICE

Least-shocking news ever: I was in my high school's show choir.

In fact, I was singing as soon as I could walk. My dad was the worship leader at our church as I was growing up, and my parents tell a story about me when I was two and a half years old, when I sang my first solo.

Apparently, toddler Kelsey was a lot like adult Kelsey (who are very different people from the prim and proper, formative-years Kelsey—stay tuned, you'll meet all of us!). I think it was just before the offering plates were passed around when I marched myself onto the stage, commandeered the microphone, and belted out "Victory in Jesus" at the top of my little lungs.

Only I added my own (unintentional) variation to the song. If you're familiar with the hymn, you know the lyrics are "He plunged me / To Victory / Beneath the cleansing flood." Except toddler Kelsey sang, "He *punched* me / To Victory / Beneath the cleansing flood." I mean, honestly, sometimes I feel like being punched to victory feels a lot more accurate than the original.

A few years later, I was riding around with my dad and we were listening to a song we knew and we were both singing along. He turned to me and had a strange look on his face. "Babe, you know you're singing a *harmony*, right?"

I had no idea what he meant. Basically, I was singing a different note on top of the melody. And it sounded good. Really good, according to my dad. We got home and he immediately told my mom, "You're never going to believe what Kelsey did. She sang a *harmony*. All by herself. It was amazing. She has an ear for music. She has a gift."

It was in that moment that I started paying attention to my voice and realized that maybe singing was something I was actually good at.

I continued to sing in church and school, knowing I was pretty good at it, but not qualifying my talent as much more than that—just something that came naturally to me that I enjoyed doing.

Then, in high school, enter Mr. Gemar. Mr. Gemar changed the dang game. Have you ever had a teacher who altered the course of your life? Whose words and encouragement transformed the way you saw yourself and your future? My choir teacher, Mr. Gemar, was that for me.

I remember so clearly the day he pulled me aside. I was doing a solo for some competition or another, and he sat me down after rehearsals. I had been told my entire life that I could sing, but

Mr. Gemar elevated the compliment to a vision. He was the first person to look me in the eye and say, "Kelsey. This is what you were made to do. There's something different about you. You've got *it*. The *it* factor. You can do this. You have what it takes to make music professionally for the rest of your life."

His words sparked a flame in my soul. A flame that soon became a roaring fire of passion for all things music. He's the reason I pursued music in college. The reason I auditioned for the girls' group. Probably part of the reason I do music professionally to this day. So, Mr. Gemar, if you're reading this, *thank you*. Thank you, thank you, thank you!

Isn't it amazing what one person's belief in someone else has the power to do?

So, for the next four years, I did all things music—jazz, show choir, theater musicals. I went to a highly ranked high school in central Illinois where the arts were a community priority. At my school, music and sports were not mutually exclusive. Football stars were also in show choir. The lead in the school play could also be the all-American star on the soccer team. Social lines weren't drawn the same way they are in most high schools.

I think this is when my penchant for performance shifted from pleasing others to entertaining others. I loved it. I knew I wanted to sing professionally, and I wasn't interested in considering anything else for my future profession.

But I was still a good girl in high school. I still hadn't had a boyfriend, but I did start noticing boys. Of course, I didn't tell anyone. Boys had the potential to make me bad, right? Evil! I had always told myself that relationships with the opposite sex would subject me to sin I wasn't ready to dive into. I never even had a pretend boyfriend. You know, the kid in first grade who kissed you on the cheek on the playground and then ran away? Nope. Not for me.

I struggled with the fear of changing the way that others viewed me—the fear of growing up. Instead of embracing milestones, I avoided them, terrified of not being my parents' little girl anymore.

In fact, when I was in seventh grade, I landed the lead role of Sarah Brown in the play *Guys and Dolls*. (If you're familiar with the show, you know how appropriate this casting was, as Sarah is the upstanding good girl on a mission.) One scene in particular called for a kiss between Sarah and the male lead, Sky Masterson. The director of my school's drama department wanted us to do an actual kiss. Not like, a total make-out session. Just a peck.

But I couldn't do it.

I was so afraid it would make me *bad*. I would be dirty after kissing a boy. I was so scared it would change me forever. I was so deathly afraid of anything physical with boys that I was literally sick just thinking about it. I couldn't eat. I couldn't sleep. The kiss darkened the corners of every thought, every moment, every day.

I expressed this fear to my parents, and they eventually came to the school and we all sat down with my director. God bless that public school drama teacher, because he calmly listened to our concerns and agreed to allow us to do a stage kiss—touching my cheek to his and making a kissy sound.

The "kiss" probably looked painfully stupid. But when I realized I'd still maintain my innocence, I immediately felt this rush of relief. I wouldn't wear the scarlet letter of shame, after all. I would still be clean. I would still be untouched. I would still be *good*.

All the way through grade school and even into college, there was always this underlying fear of boys, men, relationships—anything sexual, for sure. And as for me, I was *not* to contribute to the problem by walking around looking attractive. Nope. I was to cover up my body so as to not tempt the poor, weak men I came into contact with. They can't be expected to think logically if my knees are showing. And if I do wear a sundress or have a bra strap showing? Well, I had grown to believe that what men did then was *my* fault.

Modest is hottest, Kelsey. But is it, though? No. Of course it's not! What's hottest is a woman who *respects* herself. Who understands that sex is powerful, but that being sexual is human nature. It's how God created us—how He wired us, on purpose. I want my daughter to be proud of her body and all the wonderful, life-giving things it was created to do. That's not to say I want her walking around with her booty hanging out of her jean shorts, but I never want her to feel the same embarrassment and disgust that I felt about my own body.

So here's a question: Where did this philosophy come from? How did I become so dogmatized and progress from hating my body, my thoughts, and my natural impulses (which is bad enough) to hating *myself* so much that I'd allow a man to abuse and use me *for years* without ever once questioning whether or not I deserved it?

It goes back to the environment each of us was raised in, right? And mine was different from yours, and vice versa. For me, being raised in the Evangelical church gave me such a wonderful foundation upon which to build my life. I learned very early about the grace and love of Christ. I learned solid values that gave me a moral compass that heavily influences the way I do marriage, motherhood, career, and life in general today. The majority of what I gleaned—either through what I was taught or what I caught—was wonderful.

It's important to lead with all the great things I absorbed growing up in a conservative Christian environment.

But—and I want to tread carefully here—some of the subtle, unspoken messages of living "above reproach" that I mentioned earlier came from this same environment. For me, what I caught (more than what I was taught) was that there was a certain way to "be a good Christian." A perception that "all is well with my soul," even though—just maybe—all wasn't so good.

What I saw at times in my church experience was an inability to be honest about ourselves—or to be honest *with* ourselves. Think about this: How many pastors do you know who have stepped away from leadership while everyone in the congregation whispered behind curved palms, conjecturing and hypothesizing? How many churches have separated because of a divisive rumor or even a divisive truth? How many families have been torn apart, how many little girls shamed, and how many grown women have suffered abuse because we can't admit our humanity in public?

I'll never forget when Lysa TerKeurst (president of Proverbs 31 Ministries and Christian author and speaker) went public with her marital struggles. She actually admitted, out loud and in writing, that her husband had left the family and had committed adultery. At the time, there wasn't a pretty bow she could put on the situation. She was openly heartbroken and confused. And—*gasp*—she confessed that she was angry with God over it.

And for those of us following her story, we were like, *Yeah. That sucks. That's terrible. What are you doing, God?* But when you sit and think about it? What Lysa did was damn near heroic. It was something incredibly courageous. Unbelievably selfless. Something that so many of us Christians get wrong.

She admitted she wasn't perfect. That she didn't have it all together. That she, the founder of an entire organization built around what it means to be a Proverbs 31 wife and woman, had no freaking clue how to handle the hand she'd been dealt. She risked losing credibility, losing respect, even losing her income to just. be. *real.*

While doing research for this book, I came across the transcript of a podcast she did for Focus on the Family. She was talking about why she decided to open up and be so vulnerable to a group of people known for their rigidity and judgment. Here's what she said:

> One promise I've always made to myself is when I've gone through something hard, or something that seemed like, "Wow, this could be so much better if I just had a few other people who had been there, done that, who could help me along." I've always promised myself I would help those people coming behind me.[1]

Wow. Just wow.

My entire life, growing up, I thought a good girl quietly followed the rules. Kept a clean record and appearance. A good girl didn't draw attention to herself. But these words were never spoken out loud to me—at least not by my parents. (I will talk about my wonderful parents in later chapters, but I want to just say they *never* told me that this was how to earn their love [or anyone else's]. And when we talk openly now about my childhood misconceptions, it breaks their hearts that I thought this way.)

But somewhere along the way, I realized what Lysa TerKeurst knew: Good girls are brave. They're vulnerable. They're real and honest—willing to sacrifice and take risks so others know they're not the only ones who are imperfect, flawed, or messy.

As I said, I'm not anti-church—not at all. As I write this, we're under lockdown for COVID-19, and my heart aches from missing the connection of meeting in person and worshipping together, side by side. I should also tell you that I am forever thankful for the men and women who served at the churches I grew up going to. I'm not speaking to an individual person with my protests, but to a culture. A culture that perpetuates the very things it stands against—darkness, shame, and lies.

Of course, there is a reason the Christian culture reacted the way it did—and I use the word *reacted* on purpose. With the coming of the sexual revolution from the 1960s onward, there was a fairly radical swing away from a traditional or puritanical view of women and sex. And so the message became "It's my body, and I can be sexual with whomever I want, and there's no shame in it." The church reacted strongly, saying, "This is an evil movement. We need to lock down our children and their sexuality." In other words, there was an extreme reaction (by the church) to an extreme view of sexual liberality (in the mainstream culture).

But we all know that when law overshadows grace and mercy,

it births legalism. And legalism is the seedbed for shame. And while not every Evangelical church became shame-based in their approach to sexuality, some did. Indeed, there was and is a middle ground: a healthy faith perspective on sex. (More on this later.) But I had no clue what it was.

Though God has given me a platform, I never saw myself being an advocate for abuse victims. And I still don't see myself as one, honestly. But I do know that I can't stay quiet anymore.

I can't sit down and shut up and play nice.

I can't and I won't.

Chapter 4

DISASTER IN WAITING

Have you ever heard of the Enneagram? I know, I know. Yet *another* personality test to tell you how you should think, feel, and act in any given situation. I've taken them all, but the Enneagram is by far the most accurate when it comes to describing my exact flavor of weirdness.

(If you want to know your Enneagram type, there are many free tests online. Or check out www.enneagraminstitute.com.)

So, out of the nine types on the Enneagram, I'm a seven. And if you know anything about the Enneagram, you know that a seven has constant FOMO. We are extroverted, optimistic, versatile, spontaneous, playful, and the life of every party. Fun, right? Well, the other side of our personality is that sevens are also scattered, overcommitted, impatient, and impulsive.

So you take a seven, right? A seven whose greatest and most basic fear is being deprived of something good or fun or meaningful. A seven whose main goal in life is to avoid missing out on worthwhile experiences. And then, you put a seven in a box. A cement box with a maximum-security padlock. You tell a seven to sit down, shut up, and not make any noise. Basically that's like taking a Lab puppy and telling it to sit for hours while squirrels run by the window outside. *"Squirrel!"*

This is a recipe for disaster.

A guarantee of self-destruction.

And that's basically a short summary of what happened when I left home and went to college.

I went to a small private college in suburban Illinois. Near the end of my senior year in high school, I was wound up tight with the tension of longing for something different, but at the same time terrified of leaving the comfortable life I'd always known.

I was *the* quintessential college freshman. I left home scared but hopeful, with little stars in my eyes and dreams in my heart, ready to take on the world. I felt like I knew everything I needed to know and anything was possible.

Then I got to school and immediately realized I was totally wrong.

The university's music program was exclusively geared toward classically trained musicians, and as you might imagine, that's so not my jam. Ya girl likes to sing pop, okay? I am artistically compelled by the individuality of pop music. The ability to make a song belong to you. The freedom to create your own interpretation of a note or run.

Classical music is by definition the opposite of pop.

Because of that, I spent my entire freshman year of college

constantly auditioning for things and making nothing. Not one thing. As in *zero things*. I didn't make any of the choirs or any of the musicals—not one single thing.

I kept thinking, *Surely I'll make this one. I have to make something at some point, right?*

Wrong. My college career was kicked off by resounding rejection. In hindsight, I see it so clearly—I wasn't what they were looking for. Imagine hitting Play on a song and expecting to hear a gut-wrenching ballad by Celine Dion à la "My Heart Will Go On," but instead a beat drops and Fergie comes on in all her girl-power pop/hip-hop glory.

In every audition I walked into, I was set up for failure. They were trying to fit my round sound into their square perspective of what I *should* or even *could* sound like. But classical music wasn't me. I wasn't classically trained. I didn't want to be classically trained. And I was so tired of people telling me who I should be. How I should act. What I should sound like.

I thought college was where people found themselves. I had all these hopes and built-up anticipation that life was supposed to *start* for me once I left the nest. Isn't that how it is in the movies? On TV? Isn't college where people were allowed to just *be*?

But again, I was faced with more expectations. Expectations I didn't meet. Expectations I could *never* meet. (This, of course, was my perception—which, as they say, is nine-tenths of reality.)

In the back of my mind, I heard all the people's voices from my past. People who told me I had what it takes to make it in music. People who told me that I was created to be a singer.

People who told me I was special, I was different. As the days wore on and I continued to get *zero* callbacks, a sickening thought took root in my gut: *Did they lie to me? Did they build me up just to watch me fail miserably?*

To say I was discouraged would be a massive understatement. I mean, it was the story of my life up to that point: I was good, but not good enough. I wasn't what they were looking for. I was not *enough*.

Instead of getting sad, I got angry. I was like, *You want to tell ME how I should sing? What my actual voice should sound like? Oh, really? Well, how about this? I'm going to do it my way and I'm going to succeed, regardless.*

In other words, challenge accepted. Ironically, the same fighting spirit that got me into trouble is the same kick-butt attitude that helped me finally get real with myself. That kind of inner strength is God-given; I was born a fighter. It's just at that point in my life, I channeled that energy in unhealthy ways because of the judgmental way I viewed myself.

My entire life, the only thing I'd been good at was singing. I mean, I had been good at being *good*, but I got very little personal satisfaction from following the rules. But when I was on stage? I felt the most like *me*.

I think we can all relate to this to a certain degree. We perform, right? We put on a show. Maybe your show is success at your job. Maybe your show is being a Pinterest-active mom. Maybe your show is your two-a-day workouts. We get affirmed through our show. We schedule our day, our calendar, our *life* around making sure we have time and space to put on our show. And it's not necessarily bad, but take away our show? And we don't know who we are anymore. Because our show has become our identity. Without it? We're floundering—untethered and anxious and not at all whole.

At least, that's what happened to me.

All I wanted was for someone (other than my parents because, c'mon, they had to think I was the best!) to look at me and say, "You know what? You're worth investing in. You're worth giving a chance. You don't have to perform the way others do. You can just be you. You can just be Kelsey. You're worth hearing out. You. Have. Worth."

But that didn't happen. And as the saying goes, hindsight is 20/20. I can see now how the college was structured with a classical music curriculum and discipline in mind. There's certainly nothing wrong with that. But my perception was that they were rejecting *me*, when in fact, I simply didn't fit *the university's* approach to music. That happened to me so much when I was in my early twenties—because of this inner dialogue peppered with perfectionism and shame, I saw the world as judgmental. It was like I was wearing invisible glasses with lenses that made the world seem more condemning than it actually was.

And then I met a boy.

Isn't that how every story like this starts?

There are two boys, actually. One, my first real boyfriend, Mark (not his real name). The other, my ex-fiancé, Chris.

My relationship experiences up until that point had been next to nothing. I *had* a childhood crush—one that lasted from the time I was five years old until I went to college. It was one of those things where our parents were best friends and they wanted us to fall in love and have this sweet little love story. His name is Alex, and he was my very first kiss—a kiss I waited until I was sixteen years old to get.

In terms of actual *relationships*, there hadn't really been any worth noting. So, when I met Mark in college, it should come as no surprise that I had no idea what I was getting myself into.

Mark was actually a really good dude. One of the few guys I dated who wasn't a complete asshat. He was occasionally possessive and jealous, but for the most part, he treated me well. He was respectful and fun and patient with me as I figured out how to date a guy without challenging him to a tree-climbing contest or something. (This was an actual thing once, by the way.)

I did know enough to realize Mark and I were headed in two different directions in life, but I probably wouldn't have broken it off if it weren't for my attraction to Chris.

Chris was the first guy I ever really loved. Also, the man who abused me mentally and physically.

From the jump, I knew liking Chris was a bad idea. And also from the jump, I knew that I was going to make him mine.

I was coming off my first breakup when I started dropping hints to Chris. Even though I initiated it, I was still emotionally raw and feeling like crap about myself. I had also spent an entire year being told I sucked at the only thing I thought I was good at. And I was away from home for the first time. To say I was in a vulnerable state would be a joke. I was like a love-starved puppy. You could have patted me on the head and thrown me a bone, and I would have chased after it, snatched it up, and run it back to you for just a shred of approval.

But I came off as confident, as not having a care in the world. Over the years, I had become so proficient at pretending like everything was great that even I wasn't in tune with how unhealthy I was.

Everything inside of me said I shouldn't pursue the campus jock who was already in a relationship. But I didn't care. I just knew I felt this undeniable attraction to Chris. A magnetic pull that I sensed he felt, too.

⸻

I always wonder what would have been different about my life if I hadn't been in such a weird place when I met Chris. Like, it's simple math. If healthy you is a 10 out of 10, but you're at −100 emotionally and spiritually, it's going to take a freaking miracle to maintain a decent relationship. Actually, it's going to take the impossible.

Being a "good girl" hadn't really made me happy. The rules hadn't made me happy. In fact, my spiritual life was at an all-time low. I was drained—tired of being suffocated by the unattainable confines of a God who needed me to be put-together. He'd made me—created the monster inside of me that was so attracted to things I knew were bad for me. Why would He do that? Why would He give me this counter-conservative perspective just to have me wrestle it to the ground every day of my life? I was exhausted.

I had felt it in high school—the tension between what I knew was right and what I wanted to do. The two didn't line up. They never had. And I was experiencing the slow fade of faith that so many college students struggle with. I still believed. But that light of belief was dimming every single day.

So, there I was. Alone on a college campus. Questioning God—questioning everything, really. Disappointed in myself. Feeling like a total buffoon in relationships with the opposite sex. But also…I didn't feel permission to feel sorry for myself or, more importantly, truly grieve about the damaged parts of myself. I had to mask my hurt. My shame. My what-the-hell-am-I-doing confusion. Because good Christians were always thankful—always #BLESSED.

At that point, my attitude was very much *who freaking cares*. I decided that I didn't.

And then there was Chris.

Looking back, when I think about the girl who met Chris, it's hard for me to reconcile who she was compared to who I am today. When I think about that college freshman, I remember a scared, lonely, insecure little girl who didn't know how to stand on her own two feet. Who wasn't sure what she believed because she had never moved beyond the rules of religion into a relationship with the true person God is.

When I talk about how I was raised, I want to be really clear about some things.

First, my parents were and are incredible human beings and parents. They are still a huge part of my life, and I consider them both role models and friends. They took me to church and youth group whenever the doors to the church were open because they loved me. Because they wanted me to love God and know the love of God. My spiritual wounds come from a culture—not a person.

The other thing I want to be transparent about is that some of my spiritual wounds are on me. That's right—me. There comes a point in everyone's walk with God where they have to become individually accountable. Where their faith has to become just that—theirs. What your mom, dad, or grandma believe won't be enough to sustain you forever. There comes a point when you have to own your own faith.

In the book of Acts, Paul wrote to Timothy, his coworker and protégé, to encourage him to guard the heritage of the Christian faith—a faith that was being challenged by false teaching and a slanted understanding of what it meant to be a follower of Jesus.

Ring a bell? We're out here acting like we're the first generation to feel like Christianity is transforming before our eyes, but this has been going on since Jesus walked the earth. Legalism was rampant in Paul's day—not just in the culture (see the Pharisees), but even in some areas of the church.

In Acts 16, we get a little backstory on how Paul's mentorship of Timothy began.

Timothy left his family to travel with Paul, sharing the story of Jesus and establishing the early church. He became one of Paul's most trusted disciples, ministering alongside Paul as he wrote much of the New Testament.

Paul wrote this first letter to Timothy while his young apprentice was serving as pastor to the church in Ephesus.

In First Timothy, we see the depth of the relationship between Paul and Timothy when Paul addresses him as "my truc son in the faith" (1:2).

> There comes a point when you have to own your own faith.

Like, how precious is that?

Paul wanted to remind Timothy of something important: When we choose to follow God, we become part of a family and take ownership in a spiritual inheritance. It is a huge and deeply critical responsibility for every Jesus follower to recognize: We should pass down our faith to our children and to anyone God gives us influence with.

However…

Paul also tells Timothy that it's time for Timothy to step up and *own* his own faith. He says:

> Don't let anyone look down on you because you are young. Set an example for the believers in what you say and in how you live. Also set an example in how you love and in what you believe. Show the believers how to be pure.
>
> Until I come, spend your time reading Scripture out loud to one another. Spend your time preaching and teaching.
>
> Don't fail to use the gift the Holy Spirit gave you. (1 Timothy 4:12–14)

In other words, Paul couldn't hold Timothy's hand anymore. Paul couldn't be there in person to monitor Timothy's ministry. It didn't matter that Timothy was young—Paul told him to man up and set an example, but not by shoving platitudes down Timothy's throat or by challenging any idea or thought that was different from his. Paul simply told him to lead by example.

He told Timothy to read God's words. To spend time with other believers. And to rely on the Holy Spirit.

When I got to college, I'm pretty sure I believed nothing with conviction besides the fact that God existed. I had no personal opinion on the character of God. Or the Bible. Or whether or not the Holy Spirit was alive in me or if I was capable of communion with Him. That makes me sad as I write this—I grieve for that young girl at college. She had no clue how recklessly loved and pursued by God she really was.

In another part of the New Testament, Paul is as straight up as it gets. He's speaking to a diverse group of people—the church of Corinth. Instead of allowing their differences to enrich their congregation, the Jesus followers there had fallen into discord. Everybody was arguing over who was right, who was qualified to lead and who wasn't. (Sound familiar? Church culture hasn't come as far as we think, has it?) Anyway, here's what Paul says: "When I was a child I talked like a child. I thought like a child. I had the understanding of a child. When I became a man, I put the ways of childhood behind me" (1 Corinthians 13:11). In other words, at some point, you have to grow up, in life and in faith. The faith we had as a child is not the faith we should have as adults. Think about it this way—if someone gave you a jar of baby food for breakfast, lunch, and dinner, would you not starve to death? Would you not be miserable, uncomfortable, and dissatisfied? The same is true for our spiritual bodies—they need more.

Up until college, I had been spoon-fed Bible stories like infant oatmeal—only now, I was a young adult. I needed more. I had never transitioned from *knowing of* God to *actually knowing*

God. Sure, I knew the Bible like a G. I could tell you all about Jonah in the belly of the whale, the time Daniel was in a den with a lion, and how Esther courageously saved the Jewish people.

I knew all the hymns. All the parables. All the *answers*. The gospel from start to finish.

But ask me how I best connected with God? What God's thoughts were toward me? What was true about my identity and what He wanted for me? I don't think I really knew then. And I had no idea how to find those answers. It's like someone telling you about a great movie—giving you all the facts of character A and character B, but without the plot or the payoff.

For me, it was like I knew where to hit my marks on stage and what costumes to wear in which scenes, but I did not have access to the screenplay. I had content without context. Information without inspiration. I knew the what, but not the who or the why.

Again, part of this is on me. If I had been more intentional and asked more questions—if I had taken it upon myself to search for the answers—I may never have ended up with Chris in the first place.

My faith wasn't really mine.

Chapter 5

THE EDGE OF THE CLIFF

How about you? Can you relate at all? Have you ever made your faith your own? Have you ever talked to Jesus and said, "Well. It's just you and me. Let's get to know each other"? Have you made a choice to follow Jesus because you want to? Because you love Him? Not simply because of "fire insurance" and the fear of going to hell? That's fine when we are nine, but when we mature, our faith must mature with us.

For me, I was just beginning to ask some of the tough questions that all believers—at some point—have to ask themselves. Maybe not these exact questions, but similar:

If God is good, why do bad things happen?
Is drinking alcohol a sin?
If I have sex, am I ruined forever?
Is the Bible meant to be taken literally?

If I raise hell on Saturday, is it hypocritical to go to church on
Sunday?

If we don't adhere to some biblical ways of living anymore
(i.e., tattoos, women having leadership roles in the church,
divorce for reasons other than adultery, etc.), then why am
I not allowed to challenge other stipulations we still cling
to in the Word?

These are all normal, acceptable, even good questions. But I thought I already had all the answers, because I'd been told the answers my entire life. I was never challenged to figure out what I thought for myself. I was living on borrowed ideals and values, and because they weren't personal to me, I didn't have the spiritual grit to hang on to them when they started to slip away. My spiritual rock wall had no handholds.

And even if you're not sure what you think about God or the Bible, this principle still makes logical sense. When you're seven, you believe in unicorns, and it's totally chill. But when you're twenty and you believe in unicorns, you're on a reality TV show called *My Strange Addiction* with another guest who eats cat hair.

If you are like I was, if you're still trying to live off your parents' faith, there's no shame from me. But think about it—if God created us all differently, how can we expect our faith to look the same as everyone else's?

Personalizing your faith and testing your beliefs is hard work, and it's not something that can happen overnight. But Paul does give us three ways we can pursue a genuine, back-and-forth relationship with Jesus, three ways we can stop eating spiritual mush and actually challenge ourselves in our beliefs.

Here's how he puts it to Timothy: "Until I come, spend your time reading Scripture out loud to one another. Spend your time preaching and teaching. Don't fail to use the gift the Holy Spirit gave you" (1 Timothy 4:13–14).

So essentially Paul boiled it down for Timothy.

1. Read the Bible.

This has to be the most obvious way to get to know the character of God on a personal level. But here's the thing—the Bible means different things to different people. Just like I can hear a song and it makes me think or feel a certain way, my husband, Caleb, can listen to it and think and feel something completely different. Guess what? Neither one of us is necessarily wrong.

The way we respond to stories and songs has to do with how we're wired. And if God wired us, our reactions—our gut reflexes—are no better or worse than someone else's. It's our own truth. And it's a truth we have to come to on our own if we want it to mean anything to us or to anyone we try to share it with.

When people start debating certain pieces of Scripture and how their interpretation is somehow superior to someone else's, I really want to eject myself from the conversation entirely. It becomes a fruitless argument. I cling to a phrase someone very wise told me several years ago: "I trust God in you." If you trust God in me, and I trust God in you, then we don't need to fight about theology.

If you're anything like me, you might also be intimidated to read the Bible because, one, it's super freaking long and daunting. It's hard to know where to start. And two, you might feel unqualified to decipher such an ancient, revered text on your own. I'm going to go ahead and say it: Without cultural or historical context, a lot of the Bible is confusing and, honestly, really weird.

When I started digging into the Bible on my own, I started with all the things Jesus did and said. Yeah, the disciples were cool and all, but I wanted to see how Jesus acted and reacted. If He's God among us, and I want to know the character and nature of God, studying the words and actions of Jesus seemed like a good place to start.

I think if you began by doing that, you'd know more about who God is than someone who read the Bible cover to cover without pausing to ask, "Why did Jesus say that? Why didn't He yell at her? Why didn't He reject him? What's with the drawing in the sand business or making a mud-spit ball and sticking it in that dude's eye?"

You don't have to understand everything you read, but read until you understand *something*—even if what you understand contradicts what you've been taught your entire life. Grace meant something to me before my mid-twenties that changed radically when I began to realize that my expectations in life were unrealistic, that I did not have to perform to gain God's approval. Suddenly, grace went from a concept to a revelation for me. It became real, not abstract.

2. Get connected and stay connected in a faith community.

Look, I'm lazy. I mean, I work hard, but I don't like leaving my house. I'm currently nursing two of my three babies, and the thought of wearing a shirt that is made of anything besides a spandex-cotton blend gives me anxiety. Honestly, even when I'm not breastfeeding, I would rather wear pajamas or athleisure clothes every day of the week. I can't even remember the last time I put on pants that zipped or buttoned. And I feel fantastic about it.

One thing I've learned, especially since becoming a mother, is that time is elastic. There are days where time stretches slowly and painfully. The kids are whiny. My husband is out of town. Social media is ablaze with everyone knowing everything about everything. I can't lose the stupid baby weight. And my hair is annoying.

Am I the only one with days like this? I think not. Woof, I *hope* not. Time never ends on these days.

But on other days, time snaps by painfully quickly. I take my kids to the creek behind our house on the golf cart and everyone is happy. I'm fresh off a Beachbody workout, Caleb is playing with our boys in the water, Collins is sleeping against my chest, and my hair is on-freaking-point.

Time is a commodity. It's a nonrenewable resource. Time is not very forgiving, either—once this minute has passed, you'll never get another shot at it ever again.

So I get it—it's hard to stay consistently connected in a faith community because life is *life*. It's busy. It's a blur at times. And church can get really, really messy and really, really toxic. All of that is true.

But the value of being in relationships with people who want the same things out of life and faith as you do is worth every minute, every risk that it requires. It's in the context of these types of friendships that you begin to hone and fine-tune what you believe to be true about yourself, about life, and about God. Safe sounding boards are one of the best ways to ask the tough questions and wrestle with their answers.

Yes, I can go off on all the negative things about my church (or any church). We all can. We live in a consumer society—we grade, rate, and critique everything. But once you learn that God's grace is complete, and real, and beautiful, you can make the choice to look for the positive in your church. To seek out the good. It sounds corny, maybe, but be part of the solution rather than just complaining about what you think they're not doing well.

Now, more than ever, there are ways to stay connected without taking off the spit-up-stained shirt or sitting through the two-hour worship set that does more to put you to sleep these days than to connect you to God (this might be just me…#mom-life has made me choose sleep over lots of things I used to love to do pre-kids—ha!). There are *thousands* of churches broadcasting live services. But beyond that, you need individual connection. Maybe that's in the form of a small group. Maybe it's a mom group that gets together twice a month. Maybe it's even a woman in a season of life beyond yours who you ask to mentor you.

You need people. I need people. Hey, Jesus had the disciples. He needed people! Yes, He was perfect, and the disciples got a lot more out of the deal than Jesus did, but He chose to include them anyway.

If you want to grow in a faith that is your own, you need intentional, safe relationships that push you, challenge you, and love you when you need it most.

3. Rely on the Holy Spirit.

I'm not going to go into a complete and exhaustive personal statement on the Holy Spirit here. But I will tell you how this principle plays out in my life.

When I decided I was interested in the person of Jesus and realized I was being pursued by Him, I believe something about me changed. I believe God and I became deeply connected in a new and powerful way. I also believe that God speaks to me, teaches me, and convicts me through that deep connection. Some people call it intuition. Some people call it a gut feeling. It's all the same idea—we have a higher power who communicates to us through our own thoughts and feelings.

To use Paul's words, that's the Holy Spirit. Through the Holy Spirit, we can talk to God whenever we want. We can ask Him questions. We can tell Him He's a jerk. I'm not saying it's right— I'm just saying it's possible. God won't faint if you get angry with Him, I promise. Hey, He already knows you're mad anyway!

The Bible tells us that God hears us when we pray. And as weird as it may feel to talk to the ceiling or the sky, I can tell you from personal experience that prayer is a powerful, miraculous, essential practice. And if you want to get to know someone (God, in this case), you can't do that unless you *have a conversation with them*. Notice I didn't just say "You can talk to God." One-way conversations aren't really that fulfilling, right?

So, yes: I think it's possible to

> Prayer is a powerful, miraculous, essential practice.

have a two-way conversation with God that is real and authentic. How? Come with me for a second. God isn't *a being*, He *IS BEING*. Please read that again. God is not a being *among* beings, He *IS BEING ITSELF*. Let me offer some insight in case your brain is blowing apart the way mine did the first time my pastor explained this concept to me.

God is all around us. He is the very thing that holds all other things together. God *is* love. He is the manifestation of love. So when we experience true love on this earth, we're experiencing God Himself. God is everywhere, living and breathing. His creative spark is in the trees, the flowers, the wind, and the eyes of our children when they're telling us stories. The divine is among us in every way, interacting with us—if only we have eyes to see. Ears to hear. Hearts open to accept it. God "speaks" to us in innumerable ways. Through the Bible. Through other people. His ever-present Spirit is all around us. Through nature. Beauty. Children. Art. Music. Film.

If you don't have a prayer life, maybe try asking God to open your eyes to see. Ask Him to wake you up to His presence all around you. I promise you will begin to see Him in so many places you'd never expect He'd be.

If I had been practicing Paul's advice, would I have ever dated Chris? Would I have ever ended up contemplating suicide on a dark and stormy night? Maybe. But maybe not.

What I do know is that the experience that broke me also gave me the tools to be put back together again. After the hurt, pain, and shame dissipated, there was a God who wanted me to know Him. A God who wanted to know me—my heart, my mess, and my truth.

No, the end result wasn't a faith like my parents'. It wasn't a faith like my brothers', my husband's, or my friends'. It was a faith that belonged to me. And me only. And to this day, I give you my word that I'd go through it all again to know God as personally and as genuinely as I do now.

The divine is among us in every way, interacting with us—if only we have eyes to see.

Because it's that relationship—that faith—that got me through the hell that was about to come raining down.

Chapter 6

THE BEST
WORST IDEA

Have you ever watched a scary movie where someone hears a noise downstairs and they go to investigate? They're walking into a dark basement, unarmed, all by themselves, and you're screaming at the screen, "Don't do it! Turn around! Go upstairs! Or at least turn the freaking light on! Are you an idiot?!"

That's the perfect metaphor for the beginning of my relationship with Chris. There were zero good reasons for me to pursue a relationship with him. It was completely and obviously unwise, dangerous, and idiotic.

I was still a little fragile following my first-ever breakup with Mark. Breaking up sucks—I don't care what side of it you're on. You have to create a new routine, a new schedule. Those cute little texts you were used to waking up to? Gone. Even though I initiated the breakup with Mark, I was still bummed about it.

My self-confidence had just been sent through a garbage disposal of rejection. And the values and beliefs I once leaned the weight of life on were splintering under the pressure of my doubt and resistance to conformity.

Before I even met Chris, I was at an emotional deficit.

But good Lord, once Chris entered my life, I was ridiculously drawn to him. All the girls on campus were. He was *that* guy. Years of being an extolled university athlete had given him a well-rounded, strong build that made him stand out on campus. I'm just going to say it—he was hot, okay? Dark skin, dark hair, dark eyes. One thing that was also different about Chris was that he never had that unkempt, rolled-out-of-bed-and-threw-a-hat-on look most college guys have. He kept his hair cut short all the time and just looked put-together.

Did I also mention he was a musician? *And hot?*

Anyway, he was funny, well liked, and charming as hell. When he graduated, he worked in the college administration.

His parents had planted a church within a few hours' drive of the college and were viewed as pillars of the community in that area—still are. Chris was the middle of three siblings, who were also involved in the church, along with Chris. His family was a huge reason he was so well known, well liked, and almost revered on campus.

I can't tell you the first time I ever saw Chris. It was like, one day he wasn't in my life, and the next, he was. He had that sort of elusive quality, the kind where you don't even realize he's making moves and planning and scheming until you're already in the thick of it.

When I first heard of him, I was a freshman, and he was a senior. His name was constantly thrown around by girls who wanted to date him, and by guys who wanted to be like him.

But I had been seeing Mark, so this random guy everybody was getting all hot and bothered over didn't really register with me besides the vague curiosity that he couldn't possibly be as amazing as he sounded.

But by the time my freshman year was ending, our paths started crossing at random. He was involved with the school's music program, so we found ourselves in the same places from time to time.

Near the end of my freshman year, my music professors started to recognize that I could actually sing. Maybe it's because I have a naturally rebellious streak and I hounded them into submission, or maybe they just felt sorry for me—but I fought. I fought my entire college career, honestly. I continued to sing, audition, and believe that I didn't have to change my sound to blaze my own trail as a singer.

And even though I wasn't what they were looking for from a performance perspective, they understood that I had a voice and that I loved God. So, finally, they placed me on a campus worship team.

Part of being in the band meant traveling all summer to play at different camps and representing the university at the different junior high and high schools we played at. It also meant I got paid in scholarship money, which was a bonus.

But I still didn't want to do it.

I just wanted to go home that summer. I wanted to be around the familiar and reground myself. I knew I had changed that school year, and I hated it. I didn't want to be Kelsey with the questions. I wanted to be Kelsey who was solid in everything. Kelsey who knew who she was and what she was good at.

But my parents encouraged me to give it a shot. They were like, "Um, you just spent the last ten months complaining about not getting opportunities to perform, and now you have one. You should go."

So, I spent the whole summer between my freshman and sophomore year traveling and singing all over the Midwest. Looking back, I'm glad I did it. My parents were right (they usually are). It reignited my passion for music and realigned me with my childhood dream—to sing professionally. But personally, the distance *really* started wearing on Mark and me, and the relationship was going downhill fast. Like a boulder-off-a-cliff fast.

Then, there was Chris.

We played at one of our last camps in Indiana, and lo and behold, Chris was there, working. The school had sent him as a representative to recruit the upperclassmen at the camp. And we hit it off. Like, the sparks were undeniable. Lingering conversations. Long glances exchanged. All the flirting you can imagine (at which Chris was damn near professional).

Maybe it was the different setting, maybe it was that both of us were tired of our current relationships, or maybe it was just timing. But the chemistry I felt between us at that camp was electric.

I remember he asked me directly about Mark and me. I was thinking, *How does he even know who I am, much less who I'm dating?* But it was a small school, so maybe he'd just seen us around. The response that came out of my mouth was shocking to even me: "Oh, me and Mark? We're probably not going to make it through the summer."

Oh. So that's how you feel, Kelsey? Sometimes my mouth moves faster than my mind.

In other words, *The door's wide open, Chris. Come on in and stay a while.*

And Chris was all about giving me attention. I think that was a lot of it—the attention—more than anything else that was so intoxicating about being around him. I was surprised that *the man* on campus would even look in my direction at all. Not that I had a low self-esteem in general. Like I've said, I wasn't feeling like a hero at that current moment. But I mean, I'd give one of my smaller toes to have that waistline again.

It just felt good that he chose to talk to me. He had graduated, and I was a lowly underclassman. It felt too good to be true. Also, my true seven Enneagram nature was rearing its FOMO head. What was so great about this guy that he was all anyone could talk about? I've never been a take-your-word-for-it kind of girl, and I wanted to see for myself what all the fuss was about with Chris. I saw the draw, but I needed to understand it. To experience it. To experience *him* before my curiosity could be satiated.

These were the good old days, when you couldn't stalk people on Instagram to figure out their deal or make contact later. So after camp, we exchanged numbers under the guise of "Hey, if you ever need a worship leader," and "If I can ever help you out on campus," but we both knew what we were doing. We had a connection that neither of us was willing to move on from.

But after camp, things between Chris and me simmered. We may have texted a few times, but we were both playing it cool. I had ended things with Mark by then, but Chris was still with his girlfriend. Then we wound up in a worship band together that played at a church off campus every Wednesday night. So

I got my Chris fix weekly, but wasn't willing to make a bolder move yet.

I mean, I did the typical girl thing. I would take the long way between or after classes to "accidently-on-purpose" run into him. If you've ever had a crush on a dude, you know what I'm talking about. It's low-level stalking, but it's highly effective when done right.

Remember when the swine flu went around? If you don't, think COVID-19, but only 0.001 percent of the media coverage and general hysterical panic. True story: I've had both. COVID-19 *and* the swine flu. And the swine flu was far, far worse for me.

(Let the record show that I am a very clean human being. I wash my hands. Sanitize. All that good stuff. Famous flus must just love me or something.)

Anyway, I got swine flu and had to leave school because of it. I was so sick. I went home to recover. Chris was still on campus, working at the school, and he had noticed that I hadn't been around or at band practices or performances for a few weeks. I remember exactly where I was sitting in my parents' house when Chris texted me out of the blue.

Chris, ever charming as he was, shot his shot: I heard you're home sick with the flu. I hope we'll be seeing you around here again soon.

Okay, Chris. I see you, I thought. *You want to know when I'll be back to school.*

When I got better and returned to campus, it was on for me. He had admitted (in his own way) that he missed me. After that text, we started going back and forth with a little regularity. All I knew was that I was completely intrigued by him, and I wouldn't stop until I figured him out.

That's when things changed between us. And I'll be honest, my memory of some of this time is hazy. I have severe PTSD regarding this entire relationship, and I think my brain protects me from certain moments that I don't want to relive.

I can tell you that the bubbling rebellion I had been experiencing for years was heating up. It was now a rolling boil, actually. I knew I was about to cross a line, and I didn't really care. In all of our conversations, moments in the band together, and texts, I could discern one thing: Chris was not exactly what he appeared to be. There was something *off*. Something slightly sinister. But I wanted to know that I knew this. I was one of those people who had to make the mistake before I believed it was truly wrong.

One night we were texting pretty late into the evening. Chris was sick—something mild, like a cold.

In my mind, I was like, *I need to see him.* The thought had never occurred to me before, but I knew that that night was the night I was going to make it happen.

Have you ever been in that position before? Right before you make an unwise or straight-up stupid choice? You feel it. You think it through. You make a plan. You know nothing is going to stop you. So, you do it. Yeah. That was where I was. And I'm a pretty formidable force when I decide on something.

It's awful to admit (or maybe just street-smart), but I was like, *This is my chance. He's sick. His girlfriend isn't around to help him. He needs me. He's vulnerable. Maybe I'll get to see the* real *Chris tonight.*

I texted him: I'm bringing you medicine.

He texted back: No, no. You don't have to do that.

But, like, when Kelsey makes up her mind, she makes up her mind. I told him I was offering and that I knew I didn't *have* to do anything. I wanted to. I would drop off the medicine and be on my way.

So, I got in my car and went to his off-campus apartment. He lived with roommates, but everyone was asleep as I tiptoed inside. I knew how risky an idea this was. Like, any notion I had of this being an innocent friend-helping-a-friend thing dissipated immediately. It was late at night. Everyone was asleep. No one knew where I was. All the lights were off. Also, *Chris still had a girlfriend, y'all.*

We sat down on the couch in the living room/den area. I was like, *This is fine. Nothing's gonna happen in a common area. Everything's cool.*

The fact of his girlfriend was brought up pretty quickly. Probably by yours truly. I was going in for the kill.

"We're fizzling out," he said.

I digested that. They'd been fizzling for a while, according to Chris.

Then he said, "Why don't we go back to my room?"

That's the best worst idea I've ever heard, I thought. And I followed him.

Before you panic, nothing happened physically between us that night. We just lay in his bed, talking for hours. But emotionally, we took a giant step toward each other. We were whispering in the dark, touching along our sides if we shifted or moved. It was intimate.

Again, I brought the conversation back to his girlfriend.

"So, what's going on with her? If you know it's over, why haven't you ended it?"

I've never been known for my subtlety.

But Chris had a way of making complete garbage sound like God's spoken words. So when he said, "I just don't want to hurt her, you know? I can't find the words to do it," I totally believed him.

Strike one, Kelsey.

Let's be honest—Chris just wanted to feel me out. He wanted to see what it was like to be around me one-on-one before he broke it off with his girlfriend. He needed to have a solid plan B before scratching out plan A.

When I got back to my place, the sun was close to rising. I remember thinking, *Look at all that light*, but feeling nothing inside my soul but a dark excitement. The closer I got to Chris, and the more deeply connected we became, the more that darkness would grow. And grow and grow and grow until it crashed over me like a tidal wave, sweeping away any resemblance of the real me with it.

Chapter 7

HIDING IN PLAIN SIGHT

I think the darkness is what drew me to Chris. When you've been pushed into the light for so blindingly long, there's something so deliciously enticing about being in the shadows. I finally felt like I could be a mess—but a secret mess. And that's where he kept me—hidden.

Chris worked for the university, and he had just ended his relationship with another student. He was like, "Kelsey, you have to keep your mouth shut. This can't get out—not for a long time." He knew it wasn't a good look for him, and I knew it, too.

So there were a lot of clandestine meetings. Sneaking around. Stealing kisses. The habits we established from the jump were subversive. It was fast and furious, and I was absolutely down for it. I will say, there was definitely a voice in the back of my head whispering... *This is going nowhere good, Kelsey.* But at the same time, I didn't care. At least not enough to stop it. I don't know if I was desperate to be loved or if I just loved feeling desperate—which was the feeling our relationship left me with.

Chris never took me on dates. He never drove to me. We never courted. I wrapped my life around his in whatever way gave me more time with him. But as time wore on, that little voice in the back of my mind started getting louder. I noticed he never paid me much attention when we were around other people. It was only in the dark, when we were alone, that he was affectionate or attentive. I was aware that things weren't okay. Like, the shiny, sexy meet-me-in-the-parking-lot-to-make-out crap wasn't cutting it anymore.

But that's the thing about secrets. They're sexy. They're illicit. It's something that belongs to you that no one else can have. But the other thing about secrets is they make you sick. For real—there are studies that show how secrets affect the body and mind in adverse ways. For example, a 2019 article in *Scientific American* claims that keeping secrets is associated with lower well-being, worse health, and less satisfying relationships.[2]

I'm not saying all truths need to be shouted from a mountaintop. If our significant other forgets to pay the rent or mortgage on time, we don't need to Tweet about it. Though not all truths need to be shared with everyone—or even anyone—to maintain a healthy and happy life, concealing some truths is like swallowing slow-acting poison. Eventually, your insides are going to rot. And that's where I was finding myself. Losing who I was. Losing what I knew was right and wrong. And just feeling pretty damn stuck.

And I knew I wasn't (and am not) alone—we all have secrets. The question is, what do we do with our secrets? What if revealing them will hurt someone? If you've cheated on your spouse, and you're remorseful, and you have asked God to forgive you, should you tell them anyway? (My answer would be "Yes, you should tell them," with the guidance of a professional counselor. Again, if not, there's that secret hanging out there that could have catastrophic ramifications.)

How do you know whether or not you should reveal a secret? It's pretty easy, actually. The secrets that cause harm to you or others (addiction to drugs, gambling, and men treating you like their low-key hooker) are some of the types that make you sick. Those are the ones you can't hang on to—regardless of what you risk by coming clean.

And there's so much power in confession. I mean, it's common sense. You can't walk around with a ton of weight pressing down on you all day every day and expect to wake up and feel awesome. Confession is also biblical. God doesn't want us to just confess our issues to Him. Newsflash: He already knows your business. He also wants us to confess to each other. Here's what James, the brother of Jesus, says: "So confess your sins to one another. Pray for one another so that you might be healed. The prayer of a godly person is powerful. Things happen because of it" (James 5:16).

Things happen because of it.

Among the many cool things that happen when we enter into confession are that we

find freedom
regain wholeness
experience grace

receive and give empathy

and create space to be fully known.

People meet Jesus the person and not just the picture of Jesus hanging on a cross they've seen at church.

Because when you bring your secrets into the open, they lose their power over you. Something spiritual takes place. Like James said, *Things happen because of confession.*

Admitting your secrets also gives other people permission to admit their own. Instead, so many of us walk around like I did—in the middle of a mess, but unwilling to admit it. I was in denial even with myself to a certain degree—because I was ashamed. I knew what we were up to was wrong. Anything that has to be kept a secret long term cannot be right.

And I was scared. What if I lost Chris? What if this thing that I'd found and had formed an obsession about ended? So I kept quiet. I kept his secret. Our secret.

I was operating from a deficit position—nothing I did was enough. And somewhere along the way, that's how I began to view my relationship with God. It was as if my spiritual bank balance was always in the red. In the negative.

What I took away from the spiritual culture I was raised in was that we bring the filthy and unworthy rags of ourselves to this sort of "spiritual laundromat," where Jesus takes them and turns them white as snow. And that's the story that many of us were taught and told our entire lives. When we were still sinners, Christ died for us.

And Jesus *did* die for me. I believe that with all my heart. But He did not die because I was a rejected and unloved-by-God person. He died for me because He loved me *so much*. We were never any less loved.

I think that somewhere along the way, many of us lost sight of the nature of who God is. Our *Father.*

I can't fathom looking at any of my children and saying, "You're not good enough. Something has to be done to make you good enough for me to love you unconditionally." Impossible! I cry even *thinking* that thought. They are already loved no matter what. Because they're who they are—they're mine. Every night before bed when I tuck them in, I say, "There's nothing you can do to make Mommy love you less." They can become anything, they can choose anything, they can go anywhere in their lives, but that would not make me love them any less.

I adore them and I love them no matter what. And I'm only human. I'm only capable of a human love. How much more can a divine God love us? Because He's capable of unconditional love. You know, I think that we *think* we're capable of unconditional love. I like to think I am with my children, but again, we're only human, and God loves us on a scale that doesn't exist in our realm.

Many of us have adopted a way to view God as someone wanting to catch us in trouble and not catch us with His love. We have owned something that God never said about us. In fact, it's the opposite of what God has said about us. We've created entire traditions and customs

> I'm only capable of a human love. How much more can a divine God love us?

in a response to how we felt we were *supposed* to get into contact with God.

But what if that's not how God ever meant it to be?

Look at the context and culture of when the New Testament was written. The predominant cultural influencers of the time were the Greeks, with their literature, art, architecture, and religion. Even the mighty Romans borrowed and stole much from the Greeks, including their gods. Greek gods such as Zeus, Poseidon, Athena, and Apollo were jealous and angry and needed to be appeased. They were gods that demanded certain rituals and sacrifices. You had to pray to Helios, the god of the sun, if you didn't want your crops to fail. You prayed to Zeus if you wanted to avoid drought, and you prayed to Eros if you didn't want your spouse to leave you.

Even though there are warnings and clear distinctions in the New Testament about the culture of the day, there is no doubt that the early church lived and worked in a society heavily influenced by the retribution ethos of Greek and Roman religion. And I think we've made the mistake of viewing the one true God through a similar lens as the lowercase gods.

If you think about it, all religions besides Christianity teach a reward–punishment theology. And of course, even before the rise of the Greeks around 900 BC, the Jewish story was being written. For example, Abraham, the father of Judaism, was born more than a millennium before Homer (who was most likely born around 850 BC). In other words, this idea of a retribution-driven God even predates the Greeks. At the time the Old Testament was being written, in order to meet with God, there had to be a sacrifice. If God was going to hear you and listen to your requests, and if He was going to turn His ear to you, you had to sacrifice. There had to be bloodshed.

However, we need to dig deeper. We can't just throw out the Old Testament, because that would also be a mistake. God's nature has not changed! He loved His people as much five thousand years ago as He does today. There's a cool section in Romans when Paul is teaching about the Law, good works, and faith. He is basically saying that faith has *always* been a higher priority for God than good works (translation: being good, acting good).

Paul says this about Abraham: "If [Abraham's] good deeds had made him acceptable to God, he would have had something to boast about. But that was not God's way. For the Scriptures tell us, 'Abraham believed God [had faith in God], and God counted him as righteous because of his faith'" (Romans 4:2–3 NLT; parentheses mine).

It wasn't the sacrifice (or good works) that God desired most of Abraham, but a faith relationship. And nothing has changed! God's deepest desire—with you, with me—is connection, intimacy, and relationship. Not works-based acceptance.

Put another way, the sacrifice was not to earn back God's love (which never left in the first place), but to *restore relationship*. There's a big difference!

The point I am trying to make is that though God has not changed, societies and cultures have heavily influenced—and sometimes messed up—the true nature of a loving God. Think about this: God didn't love us any more deeply after Jesus came to earth. (Let that settle in for a sec.)

It's not like Jesus' coming switched on God's love light for

His children. What changed was our ability, in Christ, to more fully enter into a love relationship with the Creator. Jesus showed us the way; He showed us how to love. He showed and modeled grace everywhere He went.

I don't think our faith was ever meant to be guilt driven. The Bible's view of God is much more loving than any given culture's view of Him. I mean, pick a time in history. The human-made reward–punishment systems present in every culture have always influenced that period's view of God. Think about it. During the early church it was Roman culture—brutal, dominating, and based on power and conquest. The Middle Ages? Feudalism, warfare, slavery, and conquest (not to mention this little thing called the Crusades). The Renaissance? Again, imperialism, warfare, and colonialism. Of course, there were positive glimpses of God's true nature by writers, thinkers, and saints such as Saint Francis, John of the Cross, Teresa of Ávila, and many others.

But because we're humans and we usually screw things up from time to time, we've twisted what was meant for love as what was meant for punishment. We take something that is free and beautiful (salvation, grace, freedom in Christ) and we tarnish it (guilt, shame, legalism). And that's not because we're stupid or ignorant. It's because we don't love like God loves and we struggle to understand a Father who fully knows, fully accepts, and fully wants us—messes and all. We think, *Well, there has to be X, Y, and Z. Grace isn't free. It can't possibly be free.* But it actually is. Jesus always said it like that: "My grace is free. Just accept it."

Jeremy Myers puts it beautifully:

One way that some people limit grace is when they try to differentiate between "cheap grace" and "costly grace," or start trying to limit the application of God's grace by using theological terms like "prevenient grace" or "efficacious grace." The truth is that grace ceases to be grace whenever we seek to modify or limit its application, extent, or effectiveness. You cannot cheapen grace; but you can misunderstand it.[3]

We can't quantify grace. We can't earn it. Or lose it. So why do we all walk around with shame, guilt, bitterness, and hard-heartedness like we've disappointed a God who could never see us with anything other than love?

Particularly in the past few years, I have asked myself, what if the cross was not just about erasing what humankind had gotten wrong? Instead, what if the cross was the ultimate demonstration of love, mercy, and grace? For free. Period. The end.

I am not a theologian, and I do not pretend to be one. But I have lived on both sides of grace, and I know for certain that for me, the cross of Christ has changed from being a reprimand of my failures to a reminder of the Father's love. If only I had known that when I was a freshman in college. If I had even a modicum

> Jesus showed us the way; He showed us how to love. He showed and modeled grace everywhere He went.

of understanding of that, the horror of the following years might not have ever happened.

I'm not sure who coined this phrase, but I love it: We can't possess what we don't experience. For me, it meant nearly losing my life (as you will soon read) in order to discover that the cross was fully and radically about grace.

However, as you will see, my journey back to Christ was brutal and full of detours and dangers.

Chapter 8

THE BITTY BABY FACTOR

When I was growing up, I was obsessed with becoming a mom. It ran deep to my core—beyond what a normal little girl probably feels. I was never really into Barbie dolls or even the older-looking dolls. I wanted a *baby*. Like, a baby that was *mine*. To *mother*.

Let me break the obsession down for you.

When I was about eight years old, *all I wanted on this planet* was a Bitty Baby doll. You know, the American Girl version of a baby doll. So I asked for one for Christmas. And I asked. And asked. And asked again—you know, just in case my parents hadn't heard the first 762 times. I was pretty sure I was going to get my wish, so I started preparing for my Bitty Baby to arrive. In July.

I had this off-brand changing table in my room, and I started stocking it little by little. I got one of my mom's old purses and made it my diaper bag and filled it with *aaall* the baby necessities—little diapers, empty jars of baby food, wipes, extra outfits. Apparently, I was a way more responsible mother at eight years old than I am right now!

And to step up the obsessive behavior, I would walk around my room all the time talking about how my baby was coming at Christmas. Like I was pregnant or something.

"I can't wait for my baby to get here at Christmas. My baby will be here soon. Three more months!"

I can't imagine how creepy it sounded, but I was totally into it.

Then the day came. Christmas morning. I didn't sleep one single minute. The tradition was always that we would wake up as early as humanly acceptable on Christmas morning and we knew the rules—do *not* go into the living room until we got Mom and Dad up and they went out first and made sure everything was just right and ready for us. My excitement was getting the best of me, but finally—it was time. They told us to come out and lo and behold...

There she was.

My baby. *My baby!* I picked up that baby and didn't put it back down for five or six years. Eventually, I'd get all the gear. The high chair. The carrier. The stroller. *The Bitty Baby changing table.*

Y'all. I am Bible serious when I tell you that I still own every single bit of that stuff to this day. I do. It's all carefully packed up in boxes. I tell myself that I am keeping it because I want to give it to my daughter one day. And now that I finally have one (twenty years later), I will. But I think part of me wants to hang on to my Bitty Baby because it represents something more than a toy I loved as a kid. It represents a dream fulfilled. Getting her was something I had anticipated at a manic level. I hoped for her and fantasized about what it would be like to hold her and take care of her.

And it was every bit as great as I had dreamed.

Let's look at that for a sec. God wired me to be a mom—I knew by five that I wanted to have a baby—and by eight the thought had grown from a desire to a dream. And even before I got my Bitty Baby, I already had expectations of what it meant to be a mom. Geez, even the American Girl doll commercials and ads I saw made motherhood look wonderful and easy. Perfect, actually. I mean, who *wouldn't* want to be a mom when it looked so easy on TV?

In many ways I'm still that wide-eyed little girl with her Bitty Baby. I still expect motherhood to be—if I am brutally honest—wonderful and easy. And, yes, most of the time it is wonderful. But easy? Rarely. This past weekend I was actually on deadline to finish these chapters and all three of my kids (four years old and under) decided to come down with colds. Goal not met. Nothing I could do about it.

Here's the biggest takeaway I've learned from being a parent: *Nothing will go the way you think it will, so lower your expectations and don't have lofty goals.*

I'm laughing out loud as I type that. It's obviously an exaggeration, but kind of true. Everything I said I would never do as a parent, I've probably already done. And like, tons of times too.

And, y'all, it starts the moment you get pregnant: the expectations and the how-tos, the shoulds, the do-this-and-not-thats. Eat for two—but wait, don't (you'll gain too much weight too quickly). And the expectations to

Develop a natural, drug-free birth plan.

Work out every day for a faster labor.

Have a home birth, not a hospital birth.

Use essential oils, not epidurals.

Honestly, I went into pregnancy and birth with absolutely no freaking idea how hard it would really be. Pregnancy with my first baby was a breeze, so going into the birth and delivery, I had high hopes that it would be smooth and uneventful like most of my pregnancy proved to be. *Holy Lord*, was I in for it. Birth expectations: demolished.

We had a traumatic birth story with our first son, Emmett— it's hard to relive to this day (more on that later). But the *real* struggle came *after* he was born. They tell you it's supposed to be all baby snuggles and lying around, little walks pushing the stroller, and gentle workouts a few weeks post birth.

Literally LOL. Not. My. Experience.

Post-birth expectations? Also demolished. Speaking of post birth…

Can we talk about postpartum? And how *no one talks about postpartum*? So apparently there's no owner's manual for after you push a kid out of your body, and I'll be honest—someone should really write that. Moms-to-be everywhere would eat that up. The overnight upside down that takes place the second that baby exits your body is hard to describe. All of a sudden, you go from me to we and you're now responsible for taking care of another human *life* every second of every day, having no idea what that actually means or entails.

You're adjusting to learning how to breastfeed—dealing with all the glam and glory of cracked nips, bloody areolas, leaky boobs, and a baby who wants to suck on you 24/7. You're running on zero hours of sleep—getting your days and nights mixed up because they all look exactly the same. You're eating like twenty meals a day because you're starving trying to boost your milk supply and feed a constantly starving baby who somehow manages to eat like five hundred times a day.

Did I mention you've just pushed a *watermelon* out of your lady parts (or had it cut out, c-section mamas—the real MVPs), and they send you home with some Tylenol, laxatives, diapers (for you, not your baby) and a quick good-luck butt slap from the hospital staff? You can barely walk because it feels like your insides might fall out somehow, your belly feels like a bowl full of jelly, and every urge to pee (let alone the other thing) sends you into a full-blown anxiety attack at the thought of blowing out your nether region stitches. It's a beautiful thing, having a baby.

Oh, and also, while you're dealing with all this, you're expected to know how to care for this tiny, fragile human that mostly cries, eats, and poops but looks like they could break at any given moment because they're just *so* freaking small and flimsy.

Postpartum in all its glory. Those days really are fleeting and quick in the grand scheme of it all. But I promise you, there are somehow like forty-two hours in a day those first few weeks after having a baby.

And if I thought postpartum would be easy, I was totally

in for it when it came to toddlerhood. Someone please send wine and parenting books. Actually just the wine. Who has time to read?

I mean, these three little humans I now have under my protection are just that—humans. Flawed and faulty, just like me. And again, to be completely honest, if you added up the hours I spend thinking I'm a not-good-enough mom compared to the time I spend thinking I am? Laughable—it's probably 80/20 on the "not good enough" side. (Moms, ya feel?)

Why is that? I know I'm imperfect. I know deep down I'm doing the best I can. I love these freaking kids more than life itself. So why do I spend so much time beating myself up about my shortcomings as a mom?

It's like our expectations of faith—our culture builds it up as this thing we can *accomplish*. Something we *do* that requires striving, hard work, and a grading scale so we can judge how well we are doing at it. But that's a recipe for guilt and shame, isn't it? Like, motherhood is just another success/failure journey?

But God does *not* view parenting that way. Does it take hard work and discipline (just like faith)? Yes. But is that the primary thing driving us—to be the perfect mom? What does that even look like?

Here's something that's helped me a ton: It's not either/or for God. It's *and*. In other words, we are not a good parent *or* a bad parent. We are loving *and* we lose it sometimes. We extend grace *and*, at other times, we don't.

So here's where I'm at with the mom thing: How well I'm able to accept God's grace and surrender my guilt is totally aligned with how I rate myself as a mom. Think about it. On those days when I feel crappy, mean, and inferior as a person, I feel the same exact way as a parent.

If we are wallowing in shame because we have these crazy, unrealistic goals and standards in our head about our faith, how does that affect our parenting? Don't we just project all that—good or bad—onto our kids? *Ouch.* In other words, am I doing to my kids what I was silently taught as a kid about goals, appearances, and perfection?

How much of my own expectations am I placing on my kids? Do I expect them to act and look a certain way? And when I'm in the middle of Bed Bath & Beyond and one of them pitches an epic tantrum and does the wet noodle on the floor? Am I ashamed of them or myself?

Even more reason for me to press into God as loving Father so I can then turn around and extend that grace to my kids. God knows I need as much help as I can get! I can't manufacture that grace on my own. (That would be cool, but—it's impossible.)

We are, of course, complex beings. It's the *and* thing again: We are giving and selfish, loving and mean, honest and white liars (at best). In the midst of all that complexity, we need God's grace to cut through the static and confusion—to clear away the clutter and help us recalibrate our expectations in healthy ways.

Parenting teaches me this every single day.

> We need God's grace to cut through the static and confusion—to clear away the clutter and help us recalibrate our expectations in healthy ways.

||||||||||||||||||||||||

Looking back on my completely off-the-charts excitement about my Bitty Baby, I had that same level of anticipation about going public with Chris. It was like, "When this happens, then *everything* will be great. Everything will be perfect. I just have to wait. It's coming. I just need to be patient."

And finally. Finally. *Finally.* Weeks into the relationship (if you can even call it that at the time), Chris felt like enough time had passed that we could go public.

But let me tell you. Becoming a public couple with the man I loved wasn't nearly as gratifying as getting my freaking Bitty Baby.

I noticed pretty quickly that even though we were public, Chris treated me very differently outside of closed doors than he did inside closed doors. He would never hold my hand, kiss my cheek, or touch me when we were out. When I would walk into his office during the day, there seemed to always be other girls in there. The most confounding part? He would flirt with and hug the girls who worked for him. When I would walk in, it was just like, "Hey, babe." He kept it ridiculously professional. You'd almost never know that we were dating.

But when the doors were closed? Chris turned into another person. He couldn't get close enough to me. Touch me enough. Kiss me enough. And it was always too much for me. That was the irony. I just wanted his hand on the small of my back walking into a coffee shop. He wanted me to strip butt-ass naked in his bedroom.

And look—I know how ridiculous this is going to sound, but I continued to justify his actions. Maybe I knew the truth deep down—that I was involved in something toxic, demeaning, and unhealthy. But if I knew it, I hid the truth so deep under my justifications for him that I would never admit it to myself. I just knew that I had already sacrificed and invested so much into this man that I had to make something meaningful come of it.

So I'd tell myself, *Just give him time. He'll grow more comfortable expressing his emotions in public. The affection will move from the bedroom to the restaurant. Just give him more time.*

Then I'd do something even more sick. I'd make it my fault. *Maybe he's ashamed that I'm still a student and he's a graduate. Of course. Yeah. I see why he's so standoffish around campus. Maybe he's being responsible. Maybe he's trying to protect his job.*

And I didn't push it, you know? Because I had the guy that everybody else wanted. So I was treading carefully to make this relationship work. *Don't be stupid, Kelsey. This dude is THE prize. You've won him. Be quiet and let him lead.*

I've mentioned that his family was very influential in their community. Planted a great church. And had a ton of clout. But that came at a very high price—a price that everyone in the family was expected to contribute to, including his siblings.

Let me give you some examples. When I met Chris, he had an apartment off-campus. What I didn't know is that he had another room at his parents' house. Like, the room looked untouched from his childhood. I'm talking trophies, bedspread, posters—all from when he was growing up—still totally intact. He lived in the apartment Monday through Wednesday. But he was expected to be at his parents' house (his actual home) the rest of the week in order to help his parents and get things ready for church on Sunday.

His other siblings were also expected to come back home on the weekends (the older one actually still lived there then) to do whatever needed to be done to prepare the house and the family for church on Sunday. (All of this was unspoken.)

These were three grown adults living two separate lives. Their outside-the-church-plant lives, which were normal and healthy for the most part, and on the weekends their we're-still-church-planters-at-home-with-our-parents lives. And they didn't have a choice in the matter. It was not even a conversation. It was bizarre to me then, and it's even stranger to me now.

This wasn't "Hey, we're all in this together. Everyone pitches in!" It was "You are not allowed to have a life of your own. Period. End of story."

I remember one weekend I went to help Chris and the family. Because at that point, I was silently expected to also devote my life to their church. It was one of my first trips there, but of course, Chris and I didn't share a bed. I slept in another room. So I get up one Saturday morning, and it was early—maybe 8:00 or 9:00 a.m. I wake up, stumble out of bed, and there's all this commotion going on. A flurry of activity. This was the Saturday morning the kids (adults) were expected to pitch in to clean the house.

And this wasn't a light dusting of the porcelain vases (feathers were definitely not involved). They were moving furniture and scrubbing baseboards. Chris was pushing the living room furniture around to scrub the floor. I'm clean, but I'm not *moving-couches-and-chairs-every-Saturday* clean. I mean, good Lord. I'd never seen anything like it. Literally everyone was cleaning something. This was something they did regularly. This was their routine.

And here I am, in my pajamas, rubbing the sleep out of my eyes, looking like the evil stepsister in a houseful of Cinderellas and fellas.

These were not adult children. These were robots.

The realization hit me that maybe there was a reason Chris was the way he was. He had never been shown the kind of love my parents showed me.

Needless to say, I never made the mistake again of sleeping in on a Saturday and waking up to everybody else cleaning. I made sure to set that alarm, and I jumped in with everyone else without asking a single question because it was just like, "This is what we do here." So now, I was also a robot.

But the weekends at Chris's house started creating a new problem. My parents lived three hours away, but I would still visit them all the time. But once Chris's parents knew I was with him, going home was no longer an option. Chris would say, "Babe, don't you appreciate everything my parents do for you? Don't you want to spend time there since they invest in us so much—to let them know what it means to you?" And because he had such a way of guilting me into the things he wanted me to do, I nodded and would comply, because I didn't want to appear ungrateful to his family. After all, I was going to marry this guy.

I was now in Chris's world. And it was a very big, very demanding world. I didn't have time for anyone or anything else—including my own family. My parents started asking questions, but I would shrug them off. They were heartbroken. At the time, I knew that they knew things weren't right. But I had no choice but to shut my parents out of my world because it's true—they *were* right. My world was broken and falling apart, but I had made my bed, and now it was time to lie in it. I made my choice to be with Chris, and if I wanted to save face and keep that relationship intact, I simply couldn't let my parents any closer.

Before long, there was a rift of tension between me and my folks. They were hurt. They were concerned. But I was like, "I'm an adult now. Let me live my life." And the deep truth was that if they had tried to come any closer and push me for more answers, they would've lost me altogether—and they knew that. They respected the distance I put in place out of fear that they were losing their only baby girl to a man and his controlling family. And they would've been right.

Chapter 9

ZACCHAEUS AND ME

The more involved I became with Chris and weekends at his parents' house, the more withdrawn I became from the rest of the world. I stopped going to college events or parties. I stopped hanging out with friends. I mean, between the gym, the running, and the weekends at Chris's parents', I'm surprised I didn't flunk out. Every single Friday, I'd leave my last class, pack my bags, and head to his parents'. We'd stay there the entire weekend, working, cleaning, and going to church, and we wouldn't leave until late Sunday night.

I started dressing differently. Don't get me wrong—to each her own sense of style. Most days right now I go from bedtime loungewear to daytime loungewear and back to bedtime loungewear. In reality, it's all just freaking pajamas, man. The only difference is whether or not I decide to wear a bra with it. I'm not Instagramming stories of myself at New York Fashion Week, so I'm not making a statement about what women should wear. I just think girls should put on whatever makes them feel the most comfortable and confident.

In those days, though, I went from wearing what the average college student wears—T-shirts, jeans, athletic wear, stuff you could just throw on—to wearing Ann Taylor and J.Crew on the daily. Like, it wasn't just Ann Taylor on a Sunday, but ironed and starched Ann Taylor on a random Tuesday morning with pearls and a cardigan. Obviously, I'm exaggerating a little, but you get it. That's what his mom wore, and I wanted to fit in. I wanted to belong—to be *good enough*.

All of a sudden, I needed to look just as put-together as they did. On the inside and the outside. Every Saturday night, Chris's mom would make her rounds. She'd ask us what we planned to wear to church the next day, and she'd take it from us to iron it. And I was like, *Wait. People still iron?* I mean, I'm not trying to wear something that looks like it's been in a suitcase for a year, but also, when I sit down, I want my clothes to sit down with me.

If I were to draw a picture of what this family looked like, I'd start with RT.

That's what we called his dad—RT. Which stood for Reverend Todd (again, this is not his real name). And it wasn't just his congregation that called him RT. His kids called him RT, too. Not Dad. Or rarely Dad. Just RT. That's who he was. It was his entire identity. You and me? We have more than one title, right? Mom, sister, friend, niece, whatever. Not RT. He was fully and completely Reverend Todd.

When I imagine RT, I imagine this huge eagle. Don't laugh at me—if you met the guy, you'd get this. He was like this huge eagle with his wings outstretched over all his children, his community, his church. But if you zoomed in really close on that picture, you'd see that there were many, many things RT had not just his wings around but also his talons sunk into.

I have a great relationship with my parents. I'm a huge advocate of that. Like, if you can, get along with your parents, even if it's difficult. Do what you can to make it work. My mom and I went and got our very first tattoos together. I talk to her literally every day. Especially now that I'm a mom. I'm like, "Hey, so, Collins is almost a year old and still basically doesn't have any teeth. That's cool, right?" And whatever she tells me is God's truth. But I call my parents because I want to—not because I feel like I have to.

Chris, on the other hand, couldn't do a single thing without consulting RT. I can't stress this enough—he was texting or calling his dad all day, every day. I remember one time, he had something going on at work. It wasn't a big deal. It was like, should he or shouldn't he have this conversation with someone. I counted literally eight times that Chris called his dad to get his advice. And that's just when I was with Chris that day. It was incessant.

And again, I can see the truth crystal clear in the rearview. When I was living it, I thought, *Oh, they're just super close. He just respects his dad.* But now it's obvious. Chris didn't want his dad's advice. He wanted the Reverend Todd stamp of approval. And that was a difficult stamp to come by.

No family is perfect. And I know I may sound completely judgmental here, but there were some deep-rooted issues in Chris's family that I know led him to where he found himself. And these deep-rooted issues aren't unique to his family. Every family has their own stuff. Yeah, maybe this particular family had more than the average, but when I think about Chris's family, they are a complete microcosm of conservative Christian culture and all the ways it can twist our mentality—twist our faith.

A few months into this whirlwind, RT sat me down. I remember thinking, *Am I in trouble? Did I not clean the stair railing well enough? Is there a hole in my Ann Taylor cardigan?*

RT did what RT did. He assumed I, too, wanted to put their church at the center of my orbit.

He said, "Okay. It's time that we acknowledge your gift of music and find your place in our church. I know you can sing. I would love for you to consider becoming our full-time worship leader."

At the time, they didn't have anyone in that role. People just alternated from week to week. I guess in his mind, it made perfect sense that if I was going to be in it for the long haul with Chris, I needed to step up and fill the spot.

I don't even know what I said back, but it wouldn't have mattered. The decision had been made. I remembered the conversation later on and thinking about it, like, *What just happened? What did I just agree to? Did I actually agree to it?*

The truth is, I didn't want to be a worship leader. I knew that. Chris knew that. My dreams were no secret to anyone who knew me; they had never changed. I wanted to finish school, move to Nashville, pursue music professionally, and one day be a mama.

When it came to Chris's family, nobody ever asked me what I wanted. Not even Chris. Nobody was ever like, *Kelsey, what are your dreams? What do you see for your future?* I guess that should come as no surprise. It's not like Chris or any of his siblings got to pursue what they wanted to do in life. They couldn't even sleep in on a Saturday.

Have you ever driven somewhere and arrived at the destination and been like, *How the hell did I even get here? I don't even remember driving here. That's scary.*

That's exactly how I felt when I arrived on stage as one of the worship leaders of RT's church. Because somehow, I'd managed to slip around the full-time role he'd offered me and just put in more time leading on as many weeks as I could.

Later on, I talked to Chris about it. I told him that I didn't mind filling in as worship leader as long as it still lined up with what I wanted to do in the future. But after school, I still wanted to chase the dream of having a full-time career as a singer. Which meant moving. Which meant leaving the family compound.

Chris never came out and told me no. Of course not. He was too charming and too cunning for that. He'd say, "We'll see, babe." Or "Let's just play it by ear." Or my favorite: "If that's God's will, it'll happen."

I was like a starved prisoner. Chris fed me just enough words and just enough affection to keep our relationship alive.

Ultimately, I had to decide. His way or mine. His family or mine. His dreams or mine. Choices. I had to make a choice.

There's a story I heard again in the last year or two at the church we are going to here in Nashville that changed the game for Caleb and me. It was the story of Zacchaeus, the tax collector. It's a story that I'd heard probably thousands of times growing up, but it never hit me on a personal level until my pastor taught it in the way that he did.

The story resonates with me because, okay, Zacchaeus was a short man (short people unite—I'm five foot three). He was probably unattractive. He was probably really dorky. He was probably one of those people who was like, "Eww, he's just gross." He was probably just a gross, nasty little man who cheated people out of their money. He was one of the most hated people of the time in that community. It couldn't possibly get any lower than a Roman puppet of a tax collector—and a short, ugly one at that. It was unanimous. Everybody hated this man.

Jesus came into town, and He was getting to know the people there, building relationships. In the meantime, He was basically abolishing all cultural norms because He didn't give a crap about them. He was like, "You guys are messing it up, okay? You're making faith complicated. Knock it off." He came into town and was blowing up everyone's foundational beliefs in what it meant to have a relationship with God. It was good—but I'm sure also painful for these people who had grown up hearing and learning that there were requirements to get in good with the Creator.

Again, it goes back to context. The *content* of God's love was there, available to everyone. But the *context*—a brutal reward–punishment culture where the weak are tossed aside—made it difficult for people to experience godly love. Judea was truly a brutal place. Under the iron thumb of Roman rule.

Here's what happened when Jesus came to town:

Jesus entered Jericho and was passing through. A man named Zacchaeus lived there. He was a chief tax collector and was very rich. Zacchaeus wanted to see who

Jesus was. But he was a short man. He could not see Jesus because of the crowd. So he ran ahead and climbed a sycamore-fig tree. He wanted to see Jesus, who was coming that way. Jesus reached the spot where Zacchaeus was. He looked up and said, "Zacchaeus, come down at once. I must stay at your house today." So Zacchaeus came down at once and welcomed him gladly. All the people saw this. They began to whisper among themselves. They said, "Jesus has gone to be the guest of a sinner." (Luke 19:1–7)

Jesus—the guy who has been running amok with the religious leaders of the time—was in town. He's the Original Gangster, if you think about it. The oldest of G's. Because He was a rebel during this time. He was countercultural and made zero apologies about it.

Zacchaeus wanted to see this dude. So, he climbed up a tree—which honestly, I bet was low-key hilarious to see.

Jesus was probably like, "Who's that guy who climbed into the tree when I walked into the town? Why is he in a tree?" And the people probably said, "Oh, that's Zacchaeus. He's a tax collector. He's like the actual worst. He takes people's money for the filthy Romans, and he's a cheater and a liar, and everybody hates him."

I can just picture Jesus scratching his chin, thinking, *Huh. Okay.* Maybe Jesus even took a step in Zacchaeus's direction. "Let me get to know him. I want to know who he is."

And the townspeople probably yanked Him back. Like, "Oh no, Jesus. You don't want to do that."

But Jesus, in His oh-so-chill Jesus way, was like, "No, actually I do."

I wish that I had been taught more about the culture of the time when I was growing up, because it makes the story so different and so much richer when you know how they did things in that time. Our pastor was teaching that during that period and in that culture, outside of sex, having a meal with another person was the most intimate connection that you could share with someone. You only ate with people who you really knew and loved. You only invited into your space and your home people who were worthy of being there.

Jesus goes up to Zacchaeus and says, "Hey, I want to come to your house for dinner tonight."

Can you *imagine* how Zacchaeus must have felt? Can you just picture his face? This is the guy who grew up being last pick for the oxen-herding team. This is the guy who *never* has people over to dinner. This is the guy who was probably just ogling Jesus for kicks and had no spiritual walk of his own. A Roman stoolie. A traitor. An informer.

Zacchaeus was probably looking over his shoulder, like, *Me? Zacchaeus as in, THIS Zacchaeus? Wait, He means me. Jesus is talking to me!*

Jesus issued His self-invite in front of all of the people watching who hated Zacchaeus. And, you know, you and I can feel as sorry as we want for Zacchaeus, but he was a thief. He was a crook. He took money from hardworking people. He had earned his reputation. We probably wouldn't have liked him, either. This was not like the homeless guy who stands in the same spot on the same freeway exit every day. Who knows why that man is there holding a cardboard sign. His story is a mystery. No judgment from me. But there was zero ambiguity with Zacchaeus. He was the modern-day equivalent of a scam artist who cons old folks out of their retirement savings.

Jesus walked up to Zacchaeus and tore from the roots any expectation that people had put on him. He was like, "I'm going to come to your house and I'm going to have a relationship and a conversation with you."

And can you just *imagine* the pearl-clutchers? Just absolutely *shocked* that Jesus chose to go to Zacchaeus's stinky little rat hovel. It makes me laugh. I was them, once. I was them for a long time.

Jesus went to Zacchaeus's house, and He had a meal with him. He showed him respect. He showed him love and compassion—maybe for the first time in the man's life.

Zacchaeus was so moved, so compelled after just one meal with Jesus, that he flipped the script reeeeeal quick. Jesus didn't fuss out Zacchaeus. He didn't condemn him. He didn't tell him what to do, even. He just shared a meal with a lonely man who had probably spent most of his time on this planet absolutely alone and hating himself.

Here's what happened next:

But Zacchaeus stood up. He said, "Look, Lord! Here and now I give half of what I own to those who are poor. And if I have cheated anybody out of anything, I will pay it back. I will pay back four times the amount I took." Jesus said to Zacchaeus, "Today salvation has come to your house. You are a member of Abraham's family line. The Son of Man came to look for the lost and save them." (Luke 19:8–10)

This man was like, "Wait, I want to be better, I realized that I'm worthy of being a good person because Jesus loves me when I'm bad. He loves me when I'm bad, when I'm a cheater, and a thief. Jesus loves me no matter what."

That compelled Zacchaeus. The way Jesus treated him opened up a propensity for change in this man.

Zacchaeus was like, "I'll pay everyone back what they're owed. And not just that, but I'll pay interest. I'll give them what I owe them, and I'll multiply it by four."

The fact was that Zacchaeus was different because of his encounter with Jesus. But even more, think for a second how this encounter with Jesus affected the rest of the people who watched it all go down. Don't think for a second that it didn't cause a scandal—people whispering, jaws on the floor, judgments flying around. I think Jesus had exactly that in mind—to basically trash everyone's paradigm about who and what was important in their city. Yes, it was about Zacchaeus, but it was about Jericho too.

And there are so many stories like that in the Bible—where Jesus comes into somebody's life and loves them for the first time, shows them grace or mercy or compassion when no one else did, and it changes them. From the core of who they are, it changes them.

The love of Jesus—when understood in the context of Zacchaeus's story—forces us to change. It forces us to want to be better, to want to do better. Not because we're earning His love in some sort of value transaction. But because we already have it. And *that* realization isn't transactional; it's *transformational.*

At the age of twenty-one, this concept of love in the face of sin was one I hadn't yet grasped. It wasn't one I had heard sermons on or read about—or if I had, I had not been paying attention. It was one I just didn't understand.

And maybe this was one of the very reasons that I continued to try to earn love. Earn love from Chris and earn love from God. And in the end, I made a series of choices that led me into a pit that I thought I'd never crawl out of.

Chapter 10

SEX GODS (AND GODDESSES)

S o let's talk about porn.

(Wow, Kelsey, you were NOT kidding when you said that no sacred cows graze in your pasture.)

I don't really like quoting statistics, because a lot of times they're totally skewed. They're inflated or change from year to year. But because I'm confident these are accurate (just based on my personal experience) and that they will probably (sadly) never change, I will.

A recent Barna Group study revealed that more than half the men in America watch pornography at least once a month.[4] Like, well over six out of every ten dudes you're in a Target with gets on Pornhub when their wife isn't home or is asleep. And that's not just men in general; the study broke down the groups surveyed into men who claim to be born-again Christians. The results? At least 54 percent of the guys who consider themselves to be Jesus followers say they watch porn monthly.

That's basically zippo difference, people, between Jesus guys and nonreligious guys.

Maybe you think pornography is okay, and I'm not here to tell you how to think. I've seen the harm it does up close and personal, so I'm not a fan. All I can tell you is that every single time I've been in a situation where porn was even a tangential factor, it's been life-shattering. Absolutely scrape-your-guts-out painful.

It's sad. Heartbreaking. Another study suggests that one in five youth pastors and one in seven senior pastors use porn on a regular basis.[5] That's more than fifty thousand US church leaders. What's worse? Only 7 percent of churches in our country have a ministry directed at helping men and women who have struggled with or been affected by the demoralizing effects of the $1 billion pornography industry.

It's an issue that's affected even my present relationship, too. But it's just something that a lot of Christians aren't willing to really be open about. No, no, no. If you have a porn issue, that's something you need to deal with on your own. We're not preaching much about it from pulpits, or even talking about it on our ministry blogs or social media outlets. It's very hush-hush. Which makes absolutely zero sense, because obviously *most of us sitting in church are in some way dealing with pornography problems.*

Anyway, at some point in our relationship, Chris confessed to me that he had watched porn and that he felt awful about it. But when he told me, he made it seem like his struggle had been something in his past. It wasn't a big deal anymore. He was good now.

I should have known better. Because it definitely, *definitely* wasn't something he was "good" with then. And it's with this confession that the most twisted, the most sickening part of our relationship began.

Chris had already had sex in previous relationships, but I was still a virgin. Like, obviously. I was the most virgin-virgin that I knew. If you were raised in the church, it was probably similar with you: I was taught that sex outside of marriage was wrong. But not just wrong—one of the worst sins out there (more on this in a minute).

I remember one time, a student pastor of mine gave this illustration. He brought a soda can onto the stage and he told us to imagine that the soda can was our virginity. Sealed, the soda can was fresh. It was desirable. It was something people would want to pick up and open. But once popped and left to sit? That soda can was like warm tap water that nobody would ever want to drink again.

It makes me laugh now. Like, how demeaning! How disheartening for anyone in the room whose "soda tab" had been popped. No, sex is way, way more complicated—and precious—than a soft drink can. I am not grandstanding about "purity" or abstinence here. Neither am I saying that we should all toss our panties in the air and give free love a try. The issue of your sexuality is actually much more important and valuable than boiling it down to just "Should I or shouldn't I?" (That's between you, God, and your trusted circle of spiritual mentors and friends.)

What I want to say is that sex is powerful. Sex will make you believe things about yourself, about other people, and about the world that simply are not true. Sex means something. It's like pouring gasoline on the fire of a relationship. It ignites emotions, beliefs, and connections—oftentimes, in a counterfeit way.

Why is that?

Because the act does more than connect two people's bodies—it forms a bond between two souls. And I don't mean in simply a *Bachelor* or *Love Island* type of way. I'm talking about in a "flesh of my flesh, the two shall become one" kind of way. The Bible actually talks about it in both the Old and New Testaments (Genesis 2:24; Mark 10:5–9). The deep intimacy and vulnerability of sex is powerful because it is *way* more than a physical act; it involves our mind, will, and emotions—all the things that make up our soul.

Sex should be treated carefully. No matter what your personal beliefs are about it—and I know that those reading have a wide range of opinions on the subject—you should know that God created a beautiful, potent, life-changing connection when He created the act of sex.

Personally, I wish I could've stepped into my marriage without a heavy sexual backpack attached to me. I wish I could've experienced all of those sexual firsts with Caleb when we got married. Not because I think sex is dirty or that I was "damaged goods," but because my personal experiences with it were less than positive before marriage. Again, that's my experience—especially because I was such a hot mess when I was sexually active prior to meeting Caleb.

I was definitely not ready, nor did I realize this beautiful gift that sex was. I saw it through the lens of the environment I was raised in; it was something dirty and to be ashamed of. My folks didn't teach me that, nor did I hear it preached—it was a nonverbal but clear message in the culture, though.

And guess what? When you catch that message (in mostly

unspoken ways) for the first couple of decades of life, you bring those beliefs into marriage with you. It conditions you to think in that paradigm of either/or—either sex is good (after marriage), or it is bad (before marriage). The problem is, we soak in the "bad" message for twenty or twenty-five years, and guess what—it's hard to let that negative message go once wedding bells chime.

So, sex was a double whammy for me:

1. My beliefs about it were skewed. It was this forbidden, dirty, dark thing that made you "ungodly" and tainted if you did it before your wedding night. It was steeped in shame.
2. I was utterly unprepared for the power of it—the power God created and built into the act of sex.

I discovered the what, but not the why. And I'm still a work in progress in this area.

It's interesting, though—in my quest to normalize conversations around sex, particularly in conservative circles, I've discovered something. Even friends of mine who *did* wait until marriage have had struggles with sex. Not all of them, but most of them. The thing is, that "either/or" principle applies with sexuality as much as it does with our other faulty expectations.

Many of us who grew up in a conservative environment were taught we are either a virgin or we aren't. We are pure (pursuing purity), or we are "damaged goods." The *and* is just as critical with sex as it is with any other part of our lives where our faith intersects. In other words, God's not sitting around waiting for us to mess up and act out sexually. And when and if we do, He doesn't jump off His throne, point His finger at us, and yell, "Aha! I knew you would mess up!" That's human thinking. That's our either/or, works-oriented culture. We fall short *and* God loves us just as much.

He's our Father—and like a good Father, He wants the best for us. For me, personally, my best would have been to wait to experience all things sexual with just my husband, Caleb. I'm as sure about that as I am about the sun coming up over the Tennessee hills tomorrow. Why? Because there wouldn't have been past traumas to bring into the relationship if I had. And believe me, I placed enough condemnation upon myself and my mistakes to make up for anything even an angry lowercase god could throw at me. As the saying goes, we are our own worst enemy, aren't we?

The church teaches us this subtle message that sex before marriage—even if it's enjoyable—is ultimately a very terrible thing. We can debate that topic for ages; we all need to read our Bibles and figure out that one for ourselves (remember, we all have to make our faith and our beliefs our *own*). Is that me giving a subtle wink of approval to just experimenting with all kinds of sex before marriage? No. It's me being dead serious with you about what I've experienced along the way, the more conversations I've had.

It's as if we are told that if we drive a car before we own one, we will ruin it. So we don't. But it gets better: We are also told that we shouldn't *think* about the car, or—horror of horrors—*touch it*. We are simply told that once we own the car, we will enjoy a secret world of driving wonders that will forever alter our lives.

Then after we are married, it's as if someone throws us the

keys—with no practice, no preparation, no driving lessons—and we are expected to be perfect drivers.

And…caveat: I am *not* suggesting that it's *better* to test-drive your body before marriage.

My point is that we do need to better understand the car before we are expected to drive it. That's like sex with the person you've chosen to spend the rest of your life with—open, honest discussions are the key. Preferably, the discussions should happen *before* we get married. But most certainly *after* we tie the knot. And I will tell you why.

It all comes back to expectations.

We are expected to understand something—*sex*—that is a near-taboo, hush-hush subject even *after* we say "I do." Think about it for a sec. Isn't that outrageous?

Could you imagine inheriting a financial fortune and then being told, "Okay, now go home and open an Acorns account and have at it!" That's insane, right? Of course, we'd hire a trusted financial advisor to help us make wise decisions with our inheritance.

So why the hell don't we do that with sex?!

Get advice! Talk about it openly in terms of your expectations, beliefs, and so on. (And I do realize that frank discussions about sex are more common today in premarital counseling than they were even twenty years ago. Slow progress—but hey, I'll take it.)

There's a word for this taboo mindset in the church: *stigma*. And you know why talking about even *married sex* is stigmatized? Because for the most part, churches (and pastors) don't know how to have honest, open discussions about sex. In the

Greek *stigma* means a mark made by a pointed instrument (LOL at the sexual innuendo in that definition). By the sixteenth century the word had taken on a negative connotation, as in to be branded or marked.

I think sexual stigmatization has a couple of main roots in today's conservative culture:

1. Many pastors struggle with sexual temptation, so they may not feel qualified—or capable—to speak on the subject. According to another Barna Research report, "Most pastors (57%) and youth pastors (64%) admit they have struggled with porn, either currently or in the past."[6] So talking about sex in general, especially from the pulpit, can be very uncomfortable. (And practically speaking, even if a pastor doesn't have a struggle with porn, it's difficult to preach on in a mixed audience.)

2. We ostracize sex in our conservative environment—we seem to be in cultural denial that we are even sexual beings. It's as if we are taught (mostly silently) to be sexless before marriage, and then when we get married, we suddenly grow sexual organs and instantly know how to use them.

3. The church reacted to the sexual revolution that began full force in the 1960s. It *had* to; I get that. But then there was this reaction to shut down on the subject of sex—as a no-go topic "we just don't discuss." And yes, I am generalizing. I know there are wonderful churches that handle sex in a healthy way. I am talking about *my* experience—the environment I was raised in.

What we need—and what I wish I had had before I got married—are *mentors*. Not so much on the "how" of sex (might be better than junior high sex ed, just sayin'), but on the "what" and "why." What is it about sex that makes it so powerful? Why did God create men and women as sexual beings?

And as such, we need real-life married mentors who have already walked the road of sex in marriage. Whether you are married or not, find a married woman you respect who can openly and honestly tell you her story about sex in marriage. Will it be difficult to find someone safe who is willing to open up about their marriage bed? Probably. But it's worth it.

Again, I will go full disclosure on you: If you have serious sexual issues in your marriage, seek a professional. I'm not a sex expert—far from it. But it gets back to the inheritance analogy: For something that God made for good (sex), we need *help* to understand it.

If it is that important (and I think it is), then *get you some sex therapy, girl!* I have—on my own and with my husband. Has it made our sex life perfect? Of course not. But has it helped? Absolutely.

To compound the cultural baggage associated with sex—especially within the church—you have to factor in a spouse's sexual history. When two people with muddy sexual pasts come together, it gets messy.

Where I grew up in Illinois we were always running around near the creeks and ponds, scooping out pollywogs and crawdads, looking for critters and getting muddy. That's why many houses in the Midwest have mud rooms. (My arid-climate friends out West laugh at this, but it's true!) The mud room was where our mom made my brothers and me take off our muddy shoes and clothes, so we wouldn't drag the mud through the house.

Well, when you bring a history of pornography into a marriage, when you have previous sexual trauma, when your sexual history is riddled with pain, you need help getting that mud off. Otherwise, it's like skipping the mud room and dragging mud all through your "marriage house."

And seriously, y'all, *we do not talk about this enough in the church!* Most of us—not all, but I believe most—come into marriage with a bunch of "mud" caked all over us.

And hey, it's not like porn is just a "guy thing." That's definitely the stigma. But lots of women are watching it, too. That same Barna Group study says that more than half of women under twenty-five have sought out porn. And for me and my marriage, porn has complicated things. It has placed expectations on both Caleb and me that are ridiculously insane and unrealistic. And like I said before, I've had to spend lots of time in therapy to work through my own pre-marriage sex issues.

No, *issues* isn't even *close* to the right word. For me, the word is *trauma*.

My sexual *trauma*.

And that started with Chris.

Chapter 11

DUMP THE TRASH, LOSE THE RATS

It should come as no big shocker that Chris always wanted to push our sexual boundaries further than I wanted to. I was his virginal conquest. I'd push back but was never any match. I gave up piece after piece of myself to him, always hating the way it made me feel, but not knowing how else to navigate the pitch-black caverns of our relationship.

And just like with everything else with Chris and me, I felt pressure. I felt tremendous pressure to be who he needed me to be and to do the things that he wanted me to do. Want me to change how I dress? Done. Alter my dreams? Done. Alienate my friends and family? Done. I'd already given up so much. What was one more thing? Why not give up my body at that point?

Looking back, I see it all a lot more clearly now, of course.

And it had a lot to do with expectations. What did I expect of myself? I did not know who (or whose) I was, so my expectations were skewed at best. If you don't know who you are, you tend to bend quickly to the will of what others think you should or shouldn't be.

I was like a ship off course—my sails of insecurity were fully unfurled and would catch the wind of others' desires and devices. There was nothing to stop me from racing across dark waters toward a predictably destructive destination. I had *no anchor.* Yes, I knew Jesus, but my understanding of Him was filtered through a murky lens of legalism. He was an acquaintance, not an intimate friend. A pricker of my soul, not my loving Father.

> **If you don't know who you are, you tend to bend quickly to the will of what others think you should or shouldn't be.**

I think a lot of women today would say they've been in a similar scenario—or are in a similar scenario right now. Maybe even with their own husbands. Sex is such an important part of our culture, our lives, our estimation of who we are on the inside. As women, we want to be sexy. We want to be seen as sexual by the men we're interested in.

But when that old-fashioned "uh-oh" feeling lands, sometimes we aren't sure what to do with it.

We think, *Is it me?*

Like we talked about in the last chapter, there's this huge *vacuum* of information when it comes to sex (before and after marriage), especially within church culture. And oftentimes, pornography is a dark cloud that hangs over a lot of my married friends' bedrooms.

How in the *hell* are married women supposed to compete with the women portrayed in porn? I mean seriously, y'all! And I'm not attacking these women—that is *not* the point. But, come on—they are near perfect physical specimens. We. Just. Can't. Compete. (There's that word again—*compete*.)

I'm going to generalize a little here, but stick with me:

Porn is to guys (again, not always just guys—I'm generalizing to make a point) what perfectionism is to women.

In other words, in the conservative culture I grew up in, men feel that same pressure to perform—to succeed and be "above reproach." That same seedbed of guilt and shame is there for boys just as it is for girls—starting at a very young age. In my experience, that pressure to be perfect commonly manifests in pornography use for guys in the church. Not always, of course—but in a *lot* of guys.

So why do so many men—including Jesus-following guys in the church—use pornography on a regular basis?

Maybe you've heard this analogy: If you have a pile of trash, it will attract rats, right? (I full-on *hate* rats—even more than snakes.) If all you do is get rid of the rats and leave the trash, the rats will return. You have to deal with the trash, and then the rats will leave. The trash piles up in that dark, inner place inside many of us that says we are not enough. In that darkness of "less than," we need to dump our garbage—that legalistic, inner judge that tells us God doesn't love us because of ___(fill in vice of choice)___.

And the only way to get rid of that trash (that guilt, shame) is by bringing it into the light of God's love. And accepting His grace. And accepting it again. And again.

Trash out, rats gone.

Think about this: It's not as much about the *what* (for guys, porn; for women, the vicious cycle of comparison) as it is about the *why*—why do both men and women of faith end up in the same spiritual dead end of defeat? In other words, the thing that drives us to darkness (whichever poison we choose, be it porn, alcoholism, perfectionism, etc.) is virtually always fueled by guilt and shame.

Paul says it so well in Romans 7:15, "I do not understand what I do. For what I want to do I do not do, but what I hate to do I do" (NIV). Thankfully, the answer is the same for Paul as it is for us, and he states it so well: "Thanks be to God, who delivers me through Jesus Christ our Lord!" (Romans 7:25 NIV).

Here's something I fiercely believe we need to *talk* about, and it's how women don't have to be silent about their sex lives in their marriages. Girl, find you a friend you can be open and honest about this stuff with! We need to talk about the importance of sex counseling and therapy and getting away from the stigma that sex is "perfect" within the context of marriage. Or that it's dirty. It's neither! It will never be perfect. And it's also not dirty.

Perfection was kind of an expectation I had in my head when Caleb and I got married, and it hasn't been our experience at all. We both brought our fair share of garbage into the marriage (toxic exes, faulty thinking, crazy expectations, the effects of pornography on him, my history of sexual trauma, etc.). Caleb and I are both working to remove our own inner trash—both as a couple (in couples therapy) and in individual counseling. We are determined to exterminate all the rats of toxic thinking, the wounds of the past, and crazy expectations from our sex life. It's a fight. Sometimes it gets ugly. We get knocked down—but the critical thing is to just keep getting back up.

We women feel like we cannot compete with porn and the images our husbands have been subjected to through it. One older Christian friend of mine says he was exposed to pornography when he was four years old. He and a friend were playing in the chaparral near their California homes and stumbled on some old porn magazines in the brush. Do you know the effect porn has on a four-year-old brain? It's really sad to think about, isn't it? (My sons are near that age—this nearly brings me to tears as I write this.)

Some of our men were exposed to porn without knowing the road it would take them down. Some were victimized or molested. In our sexually messed-up culture, oftentimes it's not the fault of the guy when porn takes hold. But no matter how a man ends up using porn—either willfully or because of childhood exposure—the outcome is often the same. Pain. Heartbreak. Shame.

And for women? We feel cheated on by porn; it's this destructive, illicit mistress that haunts our homes. It sets unrealistic standards for both men and women as it pertains to sex. It causes women to question themselves—to doubt that they're beautiful, sexy, or good enough for their men.

Are we too prudish? Are we boring? Are we inexperienced in bed? Will he leave if we don't give him what he wants? What's he thinking about when he's with me? Is he thinking about me? Another girl? Is he thinking about what he's been watching online when we're at the grocery store or the gym?

As women we have all these questions. It's how most (maybe all) of us spend our days, isn't it (if we are brutally honest)? Expectations. Not just in sex, but all things. Are we performing well in *all* the areas of our lives? But this way of thinking about sex—this comparison and performance mindset—has always been a threat to the church. It's not just a problem in our modern, pagan culture. Look at what Paul had to deal with in the city of Corinth alone—a town dedicated to a sex goddess (through the temple of Aphrodite). I think Corinth would have given Las Vegas a run for its money.

The Corinthian church was struggling to change their mindset—they were fighting among themselves and falling into sexual deviance. Paul admonished them to accept a new way of thinking based on grace and love rather than judgment and perversion (see 1 Corinthians 6:9–12).

Does this sound familiar? Like, similar to twenty-first-century life?

No, they didn't have Pornhub in Jesus' time. They didn't have magazines, Instagram, or YouTube to twist sex or pervert it from what God intended it to be. But they found a way to do it in their culture anyway. The perverting of sex isn't something we came up with recently—it's been happening for ages.

Sex is murky, y'all. I'm telling you—it's *powerful*.

‖‖‖‖‖‖‖‖‖‖‖‖‖‖‖‖‖

Sometimes I wonder how people could question the existence of a Creator. Sure, there are murders and child abuse and terrible things that happen to good people every day. But when you take into account the creation itself—not the *actions* of the created—the argument for intelligent design is undeniable.

Take the human brain, for instance. A healthy human brain has a storage capacity that is virtually unlimited, throwing information around at an insane 268 miles per hour. In comparison, top speed for a high-level race car is around 230 miles per hour. You know how people say you can't use your entire brain? Untrue. Even when you're sleeping, your brain is working—symphonically orchestrating the many functions required to keep your body alive and well while you get some shut-eye.

For me, one of the most beautiful and almost magical things a brain can do is called dissociation. If the brain registers an overwhelming trauma, the brain has the ability to essentially delete that memory through a process called dissociation—or, the detachment from reality.

Have you ever lost track of hours binge-watching *Friends* or *The Bachelor*? (No? Just me?) If you've ever daydreamed while in the carpool line or gotten completely caught up in the storyline of a book, you've experienced mild dissociation.

Your brain has the ability to detach itself from an experience. During the middle of a traumatic, stressful, or fear-related experience, your brain will wander off into a corner somewhere and hide its eyes, like, "I'm not looking. I'm not looking," in order to avoid creating a vivid memory of the encounter.

What? How did *all of that* happen by accident?

I don't think that it did.

A lot of what I'm about to tell you is fuzzy. It's hazy. It's like trying to remember a dream.

I don't know how much time had passed in my relationship with Chris since going public, but things had started to get intense in the bedroom for Chris and me.

Every chance we got, we were looking for a bedroom. Even at his parents' house—for some weird reason, especially at his parents' house. It was that thrill of the illicit—the high I think we both got from "not being good." (Which, like any high, eventually goes away.) After everyone would go to bed, I'd head to the basement for Chris's. I don't even know how this started. But once it had, it was implied that it was expected.

Look, I'm not trying to pass off all the blame. Hardly. I own my part. My legs were the ones creeping down the stairs. But it was almost like I had no other choice. I didn't want to disappoint him. And what happened behind the closed door of his parents' basement bedroom would transform me from the inside out.

Physically, I didn't have much experience. But little by little, I started to make small concessions. Each compromise drove us closer and closer to the brink of no return.

That's how this works. That's actually how a lot of life's disasters occur. Not all at once. But one seemingly negligible decision at a time. Then it snowballs, right? Once you reach a certain threshold sexually, you are quicker to move on to the next.

And I remember *so* many times saying verbatim, "Chris, I am not having sex with you. Just so you know—if you're thinking we're heading that direction, no matter how close we get, we're not crossing that line."

I'm not sure where that strength came from. Maybe I knew

intuitively that Chris and I were not going to last. Or maybe a booming voice from a past sermon telling me I was irreparable if I consented to sex echoed in my subconscious. I'm sure the Holy Spirit was trying to break through my fog of confusion.

But I was clear on one thing—I was not having sex with him. He'd had sex before. But he'd told me he'd regretted it and felt bad about it. He'd say, "I know, I know. I don't want to, either."

But Chris was a puppeteer. He'd pull the strings, and I'd dance for him like a smiling, plastic-faced marionette. I believed him. Neither of us wanted to have sex, so we wouldn't.

The trust was blind. The trust was damning.

Chapter 12

DEAD INSIDE

I don't remember the first time it happened.

What I do remember is how dead inside I felt immediately after. His control over me was complete. I was isolated from my friends and family. I had developed what can only be described as an exercise or eating disorder. And I had changed basically every single thing about myself to make him happy. It was actually not unlike what people experience when indoctrinated into a cult.

Why did I go along? I wanted him to love me. In fact, I was desperate for him to love me. I wanted him to *see* me.

(Trigger warning: The next six or seven paragraphs are intense. You can skip them if you like.)

With this perfect storm in place, the first time Chris physically pushed himself on me, I didn't even really know what he was trying to do. Let me explain: He didn't force me in the typical sense of the word. He didn't come into my bed and cover my mouth and beat me into submission. I'm not going to say exactly what he did—not because I am a prude or because I don't think you can handle it. I simply don't want to be a trigger for others who have been through similar extreme trauma. Let's just say that he was determined to practice a form of sex with me that is fully and undeniably degrading to women in my opinion. Not the intended and traditional form of sex.

Writing those words spills tears.

I don't remember the isolated event, but I do remember thinking, *He's not about to do what I think he's going to do…right?*

But he did. And he would continue to do it over and over and over again.

"It's not sex, Kelsey," he'd tell me, somehow condescending and reassuring at the same time. "You're still a virgin."

Honestly, y'all. I didn't even know that what Chris and I were doing was something that people even practiced. I'd never heard of it. Sure as hell had never considered doing it. But he had—undoubtedly from what he'd seen from watching lots of porn.

But *Are we having sex?* wasn't even close to the right question.

The right question would have been, "Do you want to do this, Kelsey? Are you okay with this? Can I do this? Do you like this? Are you okay?"

There were about a hundred right questions, but the only one I was thinking was, *Am I still good?*

As I was writing this chapter, I had a powerful moment where I was able to jump back in time and experience the world as I did when I was dating Chris. Not literally, of course, but in my mind and emotions. I was able to grieve that girl who so deeply questioned whether or not she was "good." Sympathize with her. How she viewed herself, her God, even her body. And you know what? Those things are all connected.

It's like divine reverse engineering. We don't wake up and simply believe we are good. (Well, at least I didn't.) It's a process that is built with the end in mind. And even if we are oblivious to the process as we are going through it, God is not.

The reverse engineering of self-acceptance goes something like this:

1. *God made us in His image and loves us unconditionally.*
2. *If God loves us exactly for who we are, we don't have to DO anything to make Him love us more.*
3. *If we don't have to do anything to earn God's love, then we can accept ourselves.*
4. *If we can accept ourselves, it means that we can accept every aspect of ourselves, starting with our soul (mind, will, and emotions).*
5. *If our soul is God-made and beloved by Him, then we can accept the rest of ourselves—including our bodies.*
6. *If God created our bodies, and we are created in His image, then our bodies are made in His image.*
7. *And (going back to step 1) since God made us in His image and loves us unconditionally, then we can begin to love ourselves as God loves us.*

It doesn't happen overnight. Especially when we grow up in a culture that worships body image. It took me a long-ass time to get to the point where I crossed that Rubicon—where I liked myself and my body more often than I didn't. And there are still days when I take steps backward.

||||||||||||||||||||||||

One thing I noticed about Chris was how concerned he was with image. Not just character image, but physical image, too. The guy worked out constantly. He had been a college athlete and had never stopped treating his body like one. I was a naturally small girl. Like, looking back, I look at pictures of myself and think, *What I wouldn't give for those hips again.* But all of a sudden, I started wondering if maybe I were a little smaller here, tighter there…if maybe that would change the way he saw me.

Let me pause right here and say something. Probably every woman reading this is screaming at me in their heads. *You idiot! You don't ever have to change yourself for a man. Your body is a gift. You should love yourself just as you are.*

But that's obvious. We all know that body shaming is atrocious. And that we're our own worst critics. But the truth is, we *all* have body insecurities, no matter our shape and size. Have you ever reached a place where you're like, "Yup. I can stop working out now. Everything is perfect"? No. It's a total cultural situation that we're all way too familiar with. And we'll wear our SELF-LOVE T-shirts but still agonize over our appearance in pictures and avoid the mirror when we get out of the shower. I wish I could tell you how to solve this problem, but I can't. I'm still currently struggling to get off the baby weight from my last pregnancy, and it's making me bananas.

It was less about my jean size and more about what I wanted in response from Chris. And maybe that's why we all judge ourselves so harshly when it comes to the scale. Because we're not getting a response from someone (maybe even ourselves?) that we want.

I didn't want to be just another girl in the room for Chris. I wanted to be the *only* girl in the room. So I started questioning. What could I do? Better? More of? Less of? Why doesn't he *see me* in the room when there are other people? You know, what is it about me that he doesn't want to own? The problem has to be me.

Before I knew it, I was counting calories like a college student counting pennies at the gas pump. I started working out incessantly. Like, in the gym twice a day, every day. I'm not a runner, but at one point, I was getting in at least five miles a day. *What?* How did I even have time for all of that? I'm exhausted just thinking about that, now. The only place I'd run to right now is the fridge. Or toilet (because three kids, you feel me?). I don't even recognize the girl I was back then. Because she don't live here no more.

But I just kept thinking, *I'm younger than he is. He's so much wiser. He must notice something about me that I'm missing. And if I can fix whatever is wrong with me, he'll love me. And he'll see me. And then we'll be happy.*

Chris's family only added to the pressure I was already feeling about who I was, what I looked like, and how I appeared. I was second-guessing the person that I was.

Maybe you can relate. You worry. You wake up at 3:00 a.m. and you rehash what you said and what you did that day. You overcommunicate. You strive. You apologize. You grow weary and exhausted from all the trying and all the thinking, because at the end of the day, you have to look at yourself in the mirror and say, *You're good; stop trying so damn hard.*

This breaks my heart. I've been there. Sometimes I still find myself there.

If you are a mom (and I realize not everyone reading this is, but come with me for a minute), think of holding your baby in your arms late at night in your favorite rocker, those innocent eyes looking up at you. If your precious child then grew up to hate you and abandon you, would you stop loving them? Would their behavior change the character of your love for them?

No.

Now think how much more your heavenly Father loves you. Perfectly. Inestimably. Utterly.

Remember one of the first Bible stories that we learn in church: In the beginning, God created the heavens and the earth. He created light. He created daytime and nighttime. He created water, the sky, land, plants, the sun, the moon, and the stars. But God saved His best for last. On the seventh day of creation, God made man and He made woman.

And He looked out across at everything He had made. Every bird, every strawberry, every blade of grass. But I'd like to think that He looked longest at His most complex, His most intimate design. Intimate because we are most like Him. Did you know that? The Bible says that we were created in the very image of God. We are a mirror to our Creator. Meaning, the qualities in Him are reflected in the fiber of our very being.

He looked at us—His people—and do you know what He said?

That it was all *very* good (see Genesis 1:31). Everything else—the sun, the stars, lemurs, tangerines, honey, sugar gliders—was good. But man and woman were *very* good.

Yes, when sin entered the equation, it changed things. Sin always changes things—it did then, and it does now. But it didn't change the creation. Just the relationship between us and God. We were still *good*. Not because we're us. But because we're *His*.

Here's another way of looking at it: Humans are the *only* creatures on the planet who can procreate in God's image (See Genesis 1:27). Wow, right? He loves and adores us so much that He gave us the ability to bring forth life that honors Him and His image. Sex is the opposite of dirty. It's the opposite of shameful.

Sex is a divine gift.

But when I was with Chris, and when it came to anything about sex, I was as lost as a goose in a hailstorm.

||||||||||||||||||||||

I can't begin to tell you the torment I went through during and following the episodes when Chris would take advantage of me sexually. I was so confused. I felt like my heart was being ripped apart at every corner by my shame, my anger, my pain, and my confusion.

So. Is it sex?

Does it matter?

In hindsight, I realize that Chris's pornography issue had spurred his hunger for sexual gratification. Like, before he first pressured me sexually, Chris had alluded to the fact that he really wanted to try this form of sex with me. I was shocked.

Completely floored. For me, that type of act has no intimacy. It was demoralizing in my eyes. Degrading. But it's totally normalized and common in porn, and so, in his eyes, it was the next best thing.

He would say, "Let's just try, Kels. Come on, babe. Don't you want to feel close to me?"

Of course I did. I told him I did.

But I couldn't find the words to stand up and say, "I absolutely will not let you do this to me."

"It won't hurt," he promised. He begged. He guilted. "It won't hurt."

He lied.

How could I think this man loved me? This man who was willing to coerce me into something so humiliating and physically excruciating?

I was so desperate for him to love me. And by that point, we were so far in. In my mind, it was a done deal. Signed, sealed, delivered, *I'm your wife, Chris.* Everyone knew about the relationship, and everyone was watching us. He was basically on staff at his parents' church, and I was leading worship there. I was a functioning member of their family, aka the Christian Mafia. I couldn't get out now.

The first time we did it, I had become so broken down by his verbal maneuverings that I knew it was coming and still didn't tell him no out loud. It was just as painful as I thought it'd be. Probably more so. Absolute agony.

I would ask myself if I wasn't clear enough when I made it obvious that he was hurting me. Maybe he couldn't see the pained, panicked look on my face or couldn't tell I was pushing him away, hoping he would catch on that I didn't want what he was doing. Maybe my body language, pushing him away and trying to turn back over, wasn't enough for him to catch on that he was hurting me. Instead, when he'd sense my resistance, he'd say something like, "Babe, if you'd relax, it wouldn't hurt so much." Apparently I just needed to succumb and let him take me over.

Always my fault. Always mine.

I imagine, though, that Chris felt some sense of responsibility. Some sense of guilt. Because after the first few times, he would text me the next morning. And it was always the same thing—some trite and pithy statement about forgiveness and love and God's unending grace. He even had the nerve to send me scriptures on some of the following mornings.

It baffled me. If my view of God wasn't already fractured, I'd be like, *Is he really using God's words to make what he's doing to me okay?* I couldn't reconcile the idea. But see, I had built up Chris in my head as some sort of demigod. As ridiculous as it sounds now, I had inadvertently made him Chris(t) in my life. Center stage. First priority.

He was a minister's son. He had graduated from a Christian college. Everyone around us loved and respected him. I wanted to believe that he was pursuing God. I wanted to believe that he was a good guy. I wanted to believe that he wasn't leading me down a path of emotional and spiritual destruction.

I'm sorry, babe, he'd text. I love you. We can start over. It doesn't have to happen again.

Every. Single. Word. Was. A. Lie.

It was almost like Stockholm syndrome at that point. I would get his texts and I would think, *Oh, maybe he is a good guy. Maybe I shouldn't say anything else. Maybe he won't make me do it again.*

Oh, but he did.

Eventually, my body adapted to Chris's actions and it became less and less physically traumatic.

But emotionally, I walked around like a carved-out cadaver. I felt like someone's property. My life had become someone else's. It wasn't mine anyway. Nothing I did or said or felt was genuine anymore. I'd given my entire life, every bit of my heart and soul to a man who only loved me from behind.

My relationship with God went from a whisper to complete radio silence.

And because I clearly felt that I'd failed on my side of the transaction, I shut down toward God. In a skewed way, I thought God was my spiritual bank, and all the checks I was depositing were bouncing. I was deep in spiritual and emotional debt to my Banker, with no repayment plan.

With one hundred percent of my being, I wanted to pursue God. But with one hundred percent of my being, I also wanted to hide from Him. I felt like there was this huge chasm between us because there was so much darkness happening in the middle. And what about all that "spiritual cash" I owed Him?

It was hard not to feel separated from God, because my whole life I'd heard that God loves us when we're good—when we can pay our bills (do good works and be sin-free). We can be close to Him if we're good. The most important thing that we can do as Christians is to be good. And I felt so very *ungood*.

I didn't know how to change it. I'd forgotten (or never really understood) that Jesus had already gone to the fullest extent to prove His love for me. So, I just stopped talking to God.

And I allowed the abuse to continue. Because I craved his love like an addict in withdrawal. When the doors were closed, I at least felt like Chris saw me. Like I mattered to him. Like I was important. When the doors were closed, I could give him something that no one else could.

And his voice was always in my head: *It's not sex.*

Today's Kelsey can see more clearly, of course. And you know what? I'm calling bull$h*#. He conned me. Used me. And whatever it was, it shattered any amount of Kelsey that may have still existed into tiny pieces.

My true image—beyond my body, beyond the desperate pursuit of perfection to please Chris—was shattered there along with any sense of who I was as a person, as a woman, as a child of God.

I couldn't see the image of myself as God saw me. That mirror was smashed into tiny shards of glass.

And it would be a long time before that divine mirror—the one into which God wants us to gaze so we can "see" the love and acceptance in His eyes—was restored for me.

Chapter 13

THE BASEMENT PROPOSAL

Everyone has a unique set of life skills, and one of mine would be the ability to quote, *verbatim*, every single episode of *Friends* that has ever aired.

I know, I know. Some girls have all the luck.

For those of you who have just been transported to Earth from some other planet that may not have heard of *Friends,* it's a sitcom that was on from 1994 to 2004 about six single friends living in Manhattan.

I have seen every single episode more times than I should probably admit. It's my go-to show. The show I can have playing in the background at all times and never get sick of. The show I watch with every newborn feeding in the middle of the night. The show I choose to binge when I need to tune out life and mentally disappear.

The jokes still land with me, y'all. It's still funny. People might say, "But you've seen that episode like ten times, Kels!"

And they are correct. But like an aged wine, it just gets better with time.

I'll never forget where I was when I watched "The One with the Proposal" episode. *Friends* was in its sixth season, and so far, all of the friends were still unmarried. But there were two of the friends who had been dating each other—Monica and Chandler. They'd known each other since high school. Chandler was Monica's brother Ross's best friend, and they lived across the hall from each other in neighboring apartments.

All season long, Monica and Chandler progress in their relationship. They move in together. They talk about their past together, their future family, all their hopes and dreams. Their love story is precious. And hilarious.

Anyway, at some point, Monica's ex comes back into the picture. The ex who could never fully commit. He takes her to lunch. He tells her she's "the one who got away" and that he wants to give her all the things he couldn't give her when they were together before—marriage and kids.

Through a series of highly unlikely but comical events, Chandler hears what Monica's ex said. He's already got a ring but has been waiting to propose because he wants it to be a surprise. He wants it to be special. He wants it to be perfect for Monica.

But when he walks into their apartment, Monica is already there, waiting on him. She's standing in the middle of the room with hundreds of lit candles around her. Then, she gets down on one knee.

I don't even have to look this up—I remember exactly what she said:

"In all my life, I never thought I would be so lucky…as to

fall in love with my best…my best…" Then she loses it and cries, "There's a reason why girls don't do this!"

Then, Chandler, in all his Chandlerness, comes over and gets down on his knee, too. He looks into Monica's eyes and says, "I thought that it mattered what I said or where I said it. Then I realized the only thing that matters is that you…you make me happier than I ever thought I could be. And if you let me, I will spend the rest of my life trying to make you feel the same way."

Then he asks her to marry him, she says yes, and the other friends burst into the apartment and they all hug and cry. I literally cry even typing out the episode, for Pete's sake.

It's amazing writing. Y'all have to watch it if you haven't already. Or if you have, watch it again. (But wait until after you finish this book. Once you start, you will be hooked.) It's right up there with the "You had me at hello" scene in *Jerry Maguire*— but that's a movie quote for another time.

That is the kind of proposal I had always dreamed about. The kind where you can remember every word of what's spoken. The kind where the two people just *know* they're meant for each other. The kind that's magical in the way that so few things in life really are.

That is *not* the kind of proposal Chris and I had.

I had just finished my junior year of college and was going home for the summer. I needed a break. A break from campus. A break from leading worship. A break from Chris (though I *dared* not tell him that). I wanted to come back to the place I last remembered being *me*. Home.

But wouldn't you know it? Chris surprised me by showing

up. One morning I woke up and my parents said, "Kels, there's someone here to see you."

It was, like, eight o'clock in the morning. I said, *Who is it? Grandma? Who else is awake?*

I come down the stairs and there he is, sitting on my parents' couch. Apparently, he had driven in the night before and stayed over at my grandma's house three doors down.

And then, at some point on his trip, I got engaged.

I really can't tell you more than that from my own memory. I know it happened in my parents' basement, though. Which is ironic. Lots of basements between Chris and me. But isn't that sad? Or is it more that it's just telling? I mean, I know what happened. I've heard my parents retell the story and Chris retell the story, but I was so disconnected that I literally don't remember it.

I remember Monica's engagement better than I remember my own.

He said some stuff and gave me a ring, I took it and said yes, and then we were officially engaged.

And then for the next nine months, everything only got worse.

We started to fight. Our relationship hadn't exactly been bunny tails and moonbeams up to then, but things between us devolved quickly. Because I actually started to feel trapped. I actually stopped living in fear that I'd lose Chris and started living in fear that I'd have to keep him. I had been white-knuckle-gripping our relationship to my chest for so long that I never had the chance to step back from it and look at it.

I wonder how many times in my life I've done that. How many good opportunities I've lost or how many bad opportunities

I've taken because I didn't have the courage to loosen my hold on what I wanted—or what I thought I wanted. Because when we hang on to things too tightly, it's all we can see. We can't see beyond it. We can't even really clearly see *it*. We're too close to it. When our lack of release keeps us from stepping back to see the full picture, we miss out on the perspective that matters most—God's.

We tend to close our fists when we are afraid. Without God's context, we try to control the content. Ultimately, however, in order to move on, we have to let it go. (Don't do it. *Don't hum the song.*)

Being engaged to Chris blew me back. Everything that happened within the context of "us" was viewed through the lens of *this is the rest of your life.* The proverbial wake-up call.

I was like, *Wait. His parents control him. His parents control his siblings. That means they're going to control me, too. I'll have to permanently take the worship leader position at the church. I'll never get to Nashville. I'll never get a chance to pursue my dreams. I'll never get to be my own person.*

The sexual nature of the relationship intensified, if that was even possible. I guess Chris figured he'd put a down payment on the cow, so the milk was his for the taking.

I remember sitting down and trying to pray and just not being able to. I'd talk *at* God, but not *to* God. I felt so freaking far away from Him. So alienated. So guilty. I felt like *my* sin was so much worse than anyone else's.

In my case I thought, *How could God love me after what I'd been doing with Chris? How could He even want me to talk to Him?* Wow. What. A. Big. Fat. Lie. But I didn't see it.

There's a story in the Bible that has radically shifted the way I think about sin now. And it's a story that I don't recall hearing much early on in my faith journey.

John 8 tells us about a woman who was caught in the act of adultery. Now, if we're working off my former sin-severity scale, this one would have been way, way up there. Like a sexual sin, but add in a few extra sin points because it was adultery and not good old-fashioned sex before marriage.

Fresh off an overnight on the Mount of Olives, Jesus gets to the temple and starts teaching to the people who have gathered there. The Pharisees did what the Pharisees did, and basically dragged this poor woman up to Jesus' feet. Citing Mosaic law, they told Jesus that the woman was supposed to be stoned.

"Jesus, this woman was caught sleeping with someone who was not her husband…Now what do you say?" (See John 8:4).

I can practically hear their whiny little ass#$^% voices.

Jesus was like, "Okay. Well, you guys are all guilt-free. You've never done anything wrong? That's cool. So, if that's true, you should go ahead and kill her. In fact, whichever one of you who has never sinned, you get the first shot at her."

One by one, each person quietly walked away until there was no one but her and Jesus.

"Woman, where are they?" he asked her. "Hasn't anyone found you guilty?"

"No one, sir," she said.

"Then I don't find you guilty either," Jesus said. "Go now and leave your life of sin."

What the what?

Jesus didn't punish her? Didn't walk her through a five-step journey to forgiveness? She didn't have to wear a scarlet letter? She didn't have to behave for a certain amount of time before she considered herself okay with Jesus again?

See—that's one of the biggest hang-ups I have with certain parts of conservative Christianity. It teaches us (even if unintentionally) that some sins are bad and some sins aren't quite so bad. Don't get me wrong—I know that some sins have bigger consequences *in our lives*. In fact, in the New Testament Paul says that sexual immorality is a sin against the temple of the Holy Spirit (i.e., our own bodies; see 1 Corinthians 6:18–20).

But why? It's not that the sin is harder for God to forgive, but that the consequences can be more damaging to us (and others). Did you catch that? It's kind of like murder. We don't need a PhD in ethics to understand that murder is worse than calling into work sick when we are just "sick" of work.

Here's the deal, though: While sins may be graded on a scale, grace is not. God's grace covers all sins. *All.*

That's the entire point of the story of the woman caught in adultery: While the Pharisees graded sins on a scale in reward–punishment fashion, Jesus does not. In the eyes of Jesus, sin is sin.

But we don't think of sin that way, do we? Even if we weren't raised in a conservative church, or even in any or no church at all. There's a societal opinion on which mistakes are acceptable and which aren't. So we all live in hiding—thinking our mistakes are so much greater than anyone else's. Or maybe it's the opposite. We think, *I mean, I've definitely got it more together than she does.* Equally destructive thinking by minimizing our own "needs work" areas.

And we subtly grade others on this manmade scale, don't we? Lori Loughlin cheating to get her kids into USC? "Guilty!" Comedian Louis CK's sexual indiscretions? "Guilty!"

But Jesus would look at all of us, and He would say, "What are you thinking? Didn't I tell you what mattered most? Love me. Love your neighbor. When you get that right, then maybe you can start worrying about the hierarchy of sin in your life."

But because we're human, we'll never perfect those two commands. And because we're human, we have no right to tell ourselves that anything we've done is beyond Jesus' ability and will to forgive.

That's worth a repeat: Because we are human, we don't have to—or need to—tell ourselves that we are beyond the reach of Jesus' love and grace.

And actually, to think otherwise is, well, kinda arrogant. (Sorry, not sorry.)

Hindsight, right? So instead of leaving my life of darkness, I decided to marry it.

> Because we are human, we don't have to–or need to–tell ourselves that we are beyond the reach of Jesus' love and grace.

Chapter 14

STIRRING SLEEPING BEAUTY

There was a flurry of parties, showers, and planning. It felt like all of it was happening *to* me, not *for* me. I had zero control. It was a slap of cold water to the face, and somewhere, somehow, the real Kelsey started to wake up.

To hear my parents tell the story of my relationship with Chris still absolutely levels me. Especially now that I'm a parent. Thinking of my own children, I can't even fathom how my parents must have felt. They saw the red flags from afar. I'd chosen Chris's family over them more times than I can count. I was so skinny and frail that a good sneeze or slight breeze would have knocked me over. And I obviously wasn't my normal, talk-too-much, over-the-top self.

They'd tell me later that they felt like they had lost me. Like I was gone to them. Their reservations only grew with time. I wasn't your typical buy-every-bridal-magazine girl. I was appropriately excited, but not Kelsey-level excited. But my parents knew that if they told me any of this, I'd revolt. I had made up my mind that I was marrying Chris, and if you know me, you know that a mind made up is as good as a done deal. At that point, I probably would have written them off.

So you know what they did? (God bless them, literally.) They did what Jesus does: They practiced the actions of love instead of preaching shame and condemnation at me. Even though it's debated whether or not Saint Francis of Assisi said these exact words, I still love the quote: "Preach the gospel at all times. Use words if necessary."

That's what my parents did. In other words, their actions did the talking.

But in my mind at that time, I was thinking, *I'm sick about this, but what choice do I have?* That's how it felt at the time. I'd lost too much. I was going to make this freaking thing work if it killed me.

But back at college, Sleeping Beauty was stirring.

I hate to say this, but it's probably true—I started picking fights with Chris. He'd make a comment about something, and I'd just be contrary. Like, "No, Chris, the sky is *green*" type of stuff.

I'm sure Chris thought I'd been possessed. Never in our entire relationship had I argued with him about anything more serious than where to eat for dinner.

But I was fearful. And as the days wore on, that fear turned into pure terror. I knew everything about everything we were doing was wrong.

So I started finding my voice a little bit. After what felt like an entire lifetime of sitting down and being a quiet, good girl, I started standing up.

And *spoiler alert*: Chris didn't like it.

I started pushing back and asking questions.

"I'm scared we're going to spend the rest of our lives at your parents' house."

"Do you care that I still want to pursue music?"

"Do you care about my dreams at all?"

"Does what I think matter?"

"Do I really matter?"

Chris killed at being able to respond in a way that sounded satisfying but promised nothing.

"Of course, I care about you, Kelsey. I'm marrying you, aren't I?"

"You're doing music now. Why would I stop you from pursuing music later?"

"No, we won't have to stay at my parents' forever."

The subtext for each of those responses was:

I chose you out of everyone who wanted me. Doesn't that prove I really love you?

You'll change your mind about your dreams once we're married and have a baby.

Because I'll be planting a church of my own somewhere. And
you'll be at my side to help.

When Reverend Todd sat us down during our engagement and offered us some insane amount of money if we had a baby together within our first year of marriage, I knew the truth. There was no way out of the compound. They wanted us there. So we'd stay. End of story. There would be no room for discussion.

My parents say they would lie awake at night, worried about me. My mom told me once that they'd both just cry—both of them. They felt helpless. But they decided to pray. They prayed every night for months on months straight. They prayed that God would systematically break down the relationship. They prayed, *God, whatever it takes. We can't do this for her. She has to do it on her own, but please, just please bring our baby girl back home.*

And their prayers were answered. Chris and I began to pull apart, ripping at the seams. Then, the thin threads between were slowly snipped, one by one.

We were engaged in May, but by December, I knew I couldn't go through with the marriage, but still couldn't say the words out loud. Chris and I got into a huge fight over the phone on Christmas, and I spent the entire day hiding from the rest of the family in my old bedroom closet, sobbing.

My mom came looking for me and found me there. I can't begin to imagine what I looked like—a snotty, swollen-eyed mess in my Christmas pajamas.

She said, "Baby, what's going on? What are you doing in here? What happened?"

I wasn't ready to tell her I didn't want to marry my fiancé—the man I'd chosen over her. And so I lied. I protected him. I made excuses for him. Like I always did.

But my mom pressed a little. She took the first step toward acknowledging the huge, giant Chris-faced monster in the room.

"You know, you cry a lot lately," she said. "You especially cry a lot when you talk to Chris."

She was careful. I could feel it—how delicately she was choosing each and every word. I mean, she had to. If defensive were measured on a scale of one to ten, I had been living life at a steady thirty-seven.

But I didn't take her bait. "No, Mom. It was just a fight. It was stupid, really. It's fine. We're fine. Everything is fine."

I'm sure she was choking on all the things she wanted to say back to me. But instead, she was like, "Okay. If you say so. We just don't like seeing you cry this much." So very…Franciscan of her.

She left me in the closet, but I couldn't move. Something had shifted between us. Something had become unveiled. *She knows*, I thought. Not about the sexual abuse, but about the toxicity that existed between Chris and me. *She knows something's not okay. But I can't tell her what's going on. They'll find out the truth. The wedding will be canceled. My daddy will go to jail for murder.*

I kept quiet that Christmas.

Fast forward a couple of weeks, and we were at Chris's parents' house one weekend (as expected). We were down in his room and got into another fight. And I don't mean a little spat, I mean I was raising my voice and yelling at Chris. It was the first time I remember *really* surprising myself. Like, *Wait, was that just me? Did I just sound like an actual grown-up?*

Chris threw some crude comment at me, and I was pissed. I got up and was ready to walk out of the room, but he met me at the door. Like I've said, Chris's a big dude. And I weighed all of a hundred pounds at the time, so I didn't stand a chance against him. He put his hands on my shoulders and he physically moved me out of the way. Then, he shut the door and locked us both inside.

I remember feeling like he slapped me. He hadn't—and he never did. But his actions had the same effect. I remember standing there, wondering why it hurt so much. Like, *Did he just place his hands on me? Was that…was that okay? Was that allowed? Did he just…What happened?"*

And I had this moment where I thought, *I'm gonna lose it. I don't know what I'm going to do. But I'm about to do something. Am I going to punch him in the face? Am I going to claw his eyes out? Am I going to scream bloody murder until someone comes down here?*

Chris must have seen my thoughts written across my face, because he moved aside and allowed me to exit the room. But the way he did it…it was almost like he wanted me to know that he had to give me permission to leave his room before I could walk out. He'd let me go, sure. But just so I knew, he could have stopped me if he'd wanted to.

I walked right out of his room and I called my mom. I was crying. "Mom," I said, "Mom, I have to come home this weekend. I have to."

"Are you okay?" she asked.

I paused before responding. "No. No, I'm not okay."

I can't remember why I didn't have my car this particular weekend, but I didn't for some reason. I straight up took the train all the way home alone, because at that point, I felt like a little girl again. I was so desperate for my parents to rescue me that I probably would've hitchhiked home if that's what got me there fastest.

My grandpa was sick and close to dying, so my parents had been planning a trip to Kansas to visit him. They got me from the train station and the three of us had a very long car ride ahead of us. Like, a solid seven hours there and a solid seven hours home. I don't know if they planned this beforehand (likely), but they brought up my relationship with Chris.

Like approaching a hungry, unpredictable lion, my mom said, "So, um. Kels. How are things with you and Chris?"

I probably shrugged. "Fine."

"What's going on? Why are you home?"

I was like, "I'm not sure. I think I'm just feeling anxious."

Inside, I wondered how much I could tell them so that they'd still let me marry him. And *let me* should be in quotes, because they had no control over it. Let's be honest. I was going to do what I was going to do. But I wanted to say *something*. I wanted to let them in. I missed them. I wanted to tell them in just enough words without them trying to save me—because I knew I couldn't be saved anymore. I wanted to tell them just enough for them to help me without helping me.

"I don't know," I said, finally. "We're just fighting a lot."

My parents didn't respond at first. They probably had no idea what they'd be "allowed" to say to me. The silence stretched out between us, taut like a rubber band. It stretched tighter and tighter until finally, I snapped.

"I'm scared that he isn't going to let me pursue my dreams. I'm scared that I'm going to spend my whole life at his parents' house. I'm scared that I won't have any choices of my own."

I stopped just short of telling them what was happening sexually.

Again it was quiet in the car.

I don't know if you've ever experienced this, but there are some moments in life that you always view as a reference point. Like, before and after this event. I call them movie moments, because when they happen, it's almost as if I'm watching them happen from outside the moment itself. This part of our conversation on a car ride to Kansas in the back of my parents' car was that for me. The entire trajectory of my life was altered, catapulting me in a completely new direction.

There are two movie moments in this story, and the first one was this.

After a long pause, my mom said, "Baby, I want you to know something. I want you to hear me say it, okay? There is no amount of money, time, or investment that we will give to this wedding that will be more important to us than you being ready. That's what matters most—that you are ready to marry Chris."

This was February, y'all. The wedding was in May. We were basically already married, it was so close. Everything had been bought. All the invitations had been sent out. I'd already been thrown showers and parties where I'd received gifts. I couldn't take all that back then. Had she lost her mind?

She went on. "This is a decision that you have to feel safe

about, Kelsey." I'll never forget her use of the word *safe*. Because never once in my entire relationship with Chris did I ever feel that—did I ever feel *safe*. "I'm not telling you to break it off with him. I'm just telling you that you have a choice. You can still marry Chris. But you don't have to do it *right now*."

And it was those two words—*right now*—those two words that changed everything for me. I literally felt a breath of hope enter my lungs. I felt like whatever elephant had been sitting on my chest for months had rolled off. Immediately, my mind started racing.

I realize now the power of that conversation. Before my mom said those words, *right now*, I had been staring at an insurmountable brick wall. Now, however, I saw some flexibility—some options. In modern neuroscience it's called the power of *yet*. I didn't have to marry Chris…yet. I didn't have to commit myself to the RT compound…yet.

Well, that car ride was a *yet* moment for me. The first step I took toward hope again.

Okay. So maybe I can buy some time. Maybe there is a chance that I don't have to do this in a couple of months. Maybe Chris and I can work on things. We can get better. Then we can get married.

I was genuinely afraid to marry Chris, but I *thought* I had to do it. (I had a brick mindset—not a growth perspective.) But if I could put it off for a few months, then maybe I could breathe. Maybe I could pause. Maybe things could improve.

"You really think so?" I asked. "I could maybe push the date back?"

Then my mom—because she's a parenting genius—just gently made light of the entire thing.

She told me about all these people she knew who had postponed their weddings for any number of reasons. She told me we could change the date on the invites, call the wedding planner, move things around. She'd handle it all, she told me.

I didn't say much more on that seven-hour drive. I just sat back and felt my chest rise and fall, rise and fall.

All that's left is telling Chris, I told myself. *Just tell him you need more time. He'll understand.*

Only, he didn't.

Chapter 15

THE ESCAPE

I hate cat naps. I'm low-key jealous of anyone who enjoys them.

Theoretically, they sound fantastic. Tune out the world for twenty minutes, wake up feeling refreshed and invigorated. The only kind of nap I want is the kind where I get to go to bed in my underwear, shut some black-out drapes, turn on the noise machine, and pass out for at least three hours.

But honestly, power naps just make me mad. And as the actual Kelsey woke up from her Chris-long slumber, she was mad, too.

Before my trip home, Chris and I had left things on a terrible note. I was hurt. He was angry. Same story, different day. When I was on the train back to school, he texted me:

We need to talk.

I responded, Yup. Because we definitely did.

He picked me up and drove us to a Starbucks. Up to that point, I still wasn't sure what I was going to say. Did I have the nerve to postpone the wedding? Would I be able to tell him the truth? That we needed to reevaluate everything? Or would the wall of my interior resolve crumble once I laid eyes on him?

So we get to Starbucks and we're sitting there, just looking at each other. Man. Am I ever glad we were in a public place when we had *this* conversation.

Remember when I said there were two movie moments in this story? This is the other one. And it's the closest thing I've ever experienced to God actually being in a room with me. If I had ever doubted the existence of the Holy Spirit, after this conversation, I never will again.

Chris started talking first—as per usual. And as the words were falling out of his mouth, all I could think was, *This is the same old sh&%. This is the EXACT same old crap.*

Chris hadn't changed. Chris would never change. But me? I had changed. I had come back to life. I had come back to *me*.

"You need to trust me," he was saying. "I am the spiritual leader of this home, Kelsey. You need to follow me. I have your best interests at heart. And if you don't believe that, then I'm telling you again, I have *your* best interests at heart. I wish you'd stop fighting it and just trust me."

I could gag now, just thinking about how sick and demeaning his words were. And I realized then that he actually believed what he was saying. That this man who had sexually abused me, belittled me, ignored me, and withheld affection from me actually *believed* he was leading me well.

Poor little Kelsey. Doesn't know who she is. Doesn't know what to do. Doesn't know where to go. Let me help her. Let me show her the way.

Then the kicker: "I really feel like you're not appreciative of my family and what they've done for you. I mean, they've sacrificed so much for us. They've offered you a job. Aren't you grateful to them? Aren't you thankful? We get to be a part of their church. We get to be a part of the family."

Suddenly, it's like I wasn't even sitting at the table anymore. It was like I had been removed from the situation completely and was thirty thousand feet above it all, watching from afar. Even in the memory of it I am watching the conversation unfold from somewhere else—another table in the coffee shop. In my mind's eye, I see a girl become startled. I see her eyebrows raise, then her head turns to the side, like, *Are you serious right now?*

But he was. I was tired and yet wide awake at the same time. I was done. Our entire relationship, all I'd been was whatever Chris wanted me to be. What his parents wanted me to be. What my school wanted me to be. What my conservative culture from childhood wanted me to be. I had lost who I was in my pursuit of everyone's expectations.

I didn't even know how I actually liked to dress anymore, much less who I wanted to marry.

Have you ever worked at a restaurant? I have. One trick they have is that they keep the lighting fairly dim. Sure, there is decent lighting over most tables, but overall, the lights are kept low. There's a reason for that. Because when everybody leaves and it's time to clean up and when those high beams come on? You see the grease. You see the caked food. You see the place for what it really is.

That's what happened next. The bright lights came on and I saw Chris for what he was—a bully. A bully and a fake. Abuser would come later, but then and there, I made a choice.

Across from me, Chris was quiet. Apparently, he had finished his homily on my expected obedience to him and contrition to his family. I didn't answer. I was quiet.

"Can you do that, Kelsey?" Chris asked me. I hadn't heard what he'd said right before, but I'm sure it was something stupid and rude. I had been zoomed out from the conversation, but I snapped back into place. "Kelsey. Do you think you can do that?" he repeated.

"No."

I couldn't believe what I heard myself say. When I tell you this, it's going to sound like an exaggeration. And I am prone to embellish, so I get it. But this is the honest truth: I felt like I wasn't in control of my own tongue. I heard what I was saying, but I didn't feel like it was *me* who was saying it.

"No." I heard myself say it again.

Across from me, the color drained from Chris's face. Those might have been the first and second *no*s he'd ever heard in his life from a girl.

"I can't do that for you," I continued.

Then it was like a huge neon sign lit up in front of me. It said, YOU DON'T HAVE TO MARRY HIM!

"I don't have to do anything," I said. "I don't have to do this. I don't have to marry you. And I'm not going to marry you."

I have anxiety as I type those words, because reliving that day is like reliving a gruesome battle. A battle I won, but a battle that cost me something, too.

His face—I will never forget it—and *his eyes*. I didn't take joy in pain then and I don't now. Chris was absolutely stricken. Just taken aback. Pure, unadulterated shock. I probably looked the same. We were both getting the news at the same time—it's over. For good. And neither of us was ready for what that meant.

With the silence between us blaring in my ears, I did what any girl would do. I snatched up my purse and I marched into the bathroom. I remember standing at the sink and having to put my hands on the counter. I was shaking. Visibly trembling. My eyes met my reflection and I sobbed as I exhaled.

What just happened? I asked myself. I don't think I even knew what I had done yet. But I also knew there was no going back.

I came out of the bathroom and stopped beside Chris. I didn't know what else to say, so I blurted, "You have to take me home, now."

He was just as flustered as I was. He tapped his pockets to find his keys. He stood up slowly and walked out the door. I'm sure we both looked a hot mess walking out of that Starbucks. Since then, I've witnessed at least three other breakups in a Starbucks. Like, what is it about coffee houses? "I'll have three pumps of vanilla, a shattered heart, no whip. Thanks."

In the car, if possible, the volume on the silence dial was turned up to a deafening roar.

Just get home, I kept telling myself. *You have to keep it together until you can get home.*

Then, about a mile away from my apartment, whatever dam of shock that had been keeping Chris quiet, splintered and broke. He yelled. He *screamed*.

"How could you? How *could you*?"

He was crying, slamming his fists on the steering wheel. We pulled into my apartment complex and instead of me being able to get out and escape his rage, Chris turned on the car's child safety locks, keeping me inside.

Control. It had always been about control for Chris. I needed his permission for everything.

"Let me *out*," I yelled at him, sobbing, hysterical, broken. "Open the *door*!"

But he wasn't finished with me yet. He continued screaming at me. I don't even know what he was saying. He probably didn't know what he was saying. I'm sure at some point, however, he realized we were in a public parking lot and people could see us. Wouldn't be wise to be seen with your (ex) fiancée yanking at the door handle, trying to get out of your car. So eventually, Chris let me go.

My adrenaline had my blood whooshing through my veins, through my head. My legs carried me through the door of my apartment, but my knees finally buckled. They were like, *Okay, we got you here, but we're done now. We need a break.*

I cried. To call it crying would be like saying the Atlantic Ocean is a big puddle of water. I sobbed. I *grieved*. I reached for my phone and called my mom. I didn't know what else to do. Only, I couldn't get any words out. Just choked howls.

"Kelsey?" Once again, I can't imagine the terror she felt. She probably thought someone had died. Someone had—Chris's Kelsey. But I couldn't say those words. Because then everything I'd just done would be true. "Kelsey, are you okay? Kelsey, tell me what happened."

Finally, I started saying, "It's over. It's over. It's over." That was all I could say.

"With Chris?"

"Yes, Mom. It just happened. It just happened, and I need you to come. Please come get me."

All of the sudden, I was her little girl again. I wanted her to come scoop me up and tuck me in and tell me that everything was going to be all right. I stayed on the phone with her while she called my dad from the other line. She told him to call my brother to come find me.

Tyler was a sophomore at the same college as me. And within ten minutes, he was there. He scooped me up off the living room floor and he carried me to the couch. All I could think was, *How am I going to live through this? How am I going to get through this?*

And we're all faced with those moments, right? The moments where we wonder, *Will I survive this? Do I even WANT to survive this?* But what choice did I have? I mean, I was in my last semester of college. I was student teaching at a high school, and I had to show up. I couldn't *not* show up.

I remember the first time I read the story of Lazarus in the Bible for myself. Lazarus wasn't just any other dude—he was someone Jesus knew well and loved as a friend. When Jesus got news that Lazarus was sick, he was like, "Eh. He'll be okay."

Don't you just love it when people say that? "It'll be okay."

No, it's not okay. It's not okay now, it won't be okay tomorrow, and it will never, under any circumstances, be okay.

That's how I felt. Like nothing would be okay again. That's how Lazarus's sisters Mary and Martha probably felt, too. When Jesus finally got to Bethany, where Lazarus and his sisters lived, Martha went out to meet Him.

"'Lord,' Martha said to Jesus, 'I wish you had been here! Then my brother would not have died'" (John 11:21).

I love how she puts it. It's just a girl way of saying, "Good job letting my brother die, Jesus. I thought you were supposed to be the Son of God—the Messiah. I thought you loved my brother. Instead, he's been in the grave four days now and you're just moseying up."

Losing a loved one is not a grief I have experienced on the level that Martha had, but I had lost a good bit of myself. I had lost my entire college experience, my identity, my innocence, my fiancé, my future.

We've all lost something. A relationship. A job. A dream. Maybe even a loss like Martha's and Mary's—the loss of someone we love. And when this happens, it flays us. It cuts us wide open and creates this pervasive emptiness that just envelops us. It's all we can feel. It's all we can know. It's physiological—you wake up in the morning and feel dread, but for a second you can't remember why. Then the grief floods back in as you remember.

Jesus looked at Martha and He simply said, "Your brother will rise again" (John 11:23).

I believe that Jesus says the same thing to us in these moments of acute agony. I believe He says, "Your [whatever you lost] will rise again." Obviously on this side of the Bible, four-day-old dead bodies do not come walking out of the tomb in their grave-clothes. But Jesus was essentially saying, "It will be restored."

Your dream will be restored. You will be restored.

Like Martha, it may not happen the way you wished it had. Your prayer may not even be answered. But God says, "I'll give you what you need in *my* time, not yours." And honestly, since He can see the full picture and we can't, aren't you glad that ultimately, we're not in control?

When Chris and I broke up, I was completely dead inside. I hadn't prayed an honest prayer in a long time. All I could say to God was "Help me. Just help me."

Sometimes, *Help* is all we can pray. But all the time, that is enough. Did you know that Mother Teresa struggled for decades with depression and self-doubt? She'd written letters to her spiritual advisor where she confessed that at times she had struggled with questions of faith. She even confided that she had suffered bouts of severe depression. She said, "Loneliness and the feeling of being unwanted is the most terrible poverty."[7]

I mean, come on! Mother Teresa? But she did. And we do too.

Even our Lazarus hearts can beat again.

God says, "I'll give you what you need in *my* time, not yours."

Chapter 16

THE DAY
I DIDN'T CRY

Those first few days post-Chris I felt like I was walking on shards of glass. What I didn't know then was that those shards—that pain—were the pieces of myself that had been shattered and scattered by the trauma I'd experienced. I had to walk through that pain before God would reassemble those pieces into the Kelsey He'd created me to be.

Every waking moment was excruciating. My brother stayed at my apartment with me. He even slept in my room—watching me, making sure I woke up every morning and got dressed. He made me breakfast and started my car. It was February, and there was snow everywhere and the ground was completely frozen. But no place was colder than the place that used to be my heart.

"You can do this," he'd tell me.

No, I can't.

"Call me when you get home from school and I'll meet you here." My sweet brother, Tyler. I can't tell you how much of his strength I lived off of during those early days. In a lot of ways, I still feel like Tyler saved my life. So Ty—thank you again and again and again.

I called my dad every morning on the drive to the school where I student taught. And I would just cry. I would cry and cry and then I would cry some more. Then, I'd pull up in the parking lot, wipe my face, put on my glasses, and hope that none of my high school music classes noticed that their teacher was a complete train wreck.

I remember one morning, weeks in, my dad was like, "Baby, listen. I know you're going through so much, but you're strong, you're resilient. And you know what? Let's just decide right now in this moment that you're not going to cry today. Just for today. And let's see how it goes. There's nothing wrong with crying. But today, let's just plan on it being a good day."

I had never thought of it that way. I was waking up every day and just wallowing in my self-pity. I didn't know I could *choose* to not cry. That I could *choose* to get up and say the day was going to be a good one. And look—I know there are times when we can't help it. Like, the tears are coming, like it or not. I cried in the middle of a Target just last week because my kids were being tiny psychos. It happens.

But I was at a point in my grieving process where it was time for me to take the next step toward healing. And maybe you're there, too. Maybe you have endured heartbreak or disappointment or loss and you're just kind of wallowing in it. That's okay. But today is the day to do something different. Just one thing. Even if it's to stop crying—just for today. Or get into real clothes instead of sweats. Or make dinner, instead of ordering delivery.

My dad said, "Kelsey. You are strong. You're not going to let this ruin you. This does not define the rest of your life. You don't see it yet, but you will. Go into the school. Don't cry. Get back in the car. Don't cry. You can do this. You'll call me on your way home, and we'll talk about how you didn't cry in the bathroom stall today during your lunch break. You got this, baby."

And I said, "Oh, okay. That actually…that actually makes sense."

Brilliant advice, right? So that day, I didn't cry. And I felt better. I felt slightly more normal. It was like putting two pieces of a puzzle together and standing back to look at it, like, *Okay. There's a long way to go. But I think I can make something whole out of this.*

But there was still a huge, glaring problem. I still had a secret. A secret I hadn't told anyone. A secret I vowed to take to my grave and beyond my grave. No one could ever know what Chris and I had done. They could never know how he had made me feel. Why?

Because what would everyone think of me if they knew?

You've thought this before, right? You've done something or said something or been through something and you think, *Gah, I hope no one finds out.* Or, *I wonder who already knows. I wonder what they think.*

And it's a very real, very gripping fear.

But it's also a very stupid fear. Why? Because the most important person already knows: God. And He's already forgiven you. So…how is that bad?

Just like I had with my fears about Chris, we metaphorically choose to cry every day and stuff our secrets because we're living our lives (*lies*, really) based on someone else's expectations.

Whose? We don't know. The proverbial *they* out there that we're desperate to hide our faces from. It's like an invisible panel of capricious beauty pageant judges who punch in their 7.5s when they don't like your evening gown.

Or maybe, for you, you know exactly whose expectations you're living under. Your mother's. Your father's. Your spouse's. Your boss's. Social media's. And we're all just freaking miserable.

But no. I couldn't tell my parents. They'd look at me differently. They'd see me differently. I would cease to be Kelsey to them and instead I'd become someone else—*something* else. I'd become what I'd *done*. Nope. Can't. Won't. This was of course a lie I told myself.

Do you remember the other thing I said about keeping secrets? It makes us sick.

My secret was like an invisible rubber band wrapped around my waist. I would dig, push, and try to drag myself forward toward healing, but each time I gained ground, I'd be snapped right back to where I had started.

My secret had made me sick. And I would grow sicker still.

ııııııııııııııııııııı

I can't say that I'm much of an outdoorswoman (at least the older I've gotten). But God decided to give me two boys, so outside we go. Our family recently got a golf cart, and I'll just throw all the kids on it and take them down to the creek and let them run wild. That's about as outdoorsy as I get. I like to feel clean and believe that air-conditioning is right up there with planes, trains, and automobiles as the best inventions of all time. Have you seen that meme of the perfectly styled 1950s mom who's saying, "I'm so glad I'm not camping"? Hi, me.

I remember this one time my husband, Caleb, and I went on a hike at a nearby mountain. I live in Nashville, but a suburb of it. And we've got mountains. This wasn't a mountain-mountain—it was more like a really big hill.

And I was like, "I can do this. I can hike stuff. I'm in shape."

And it probably would have been fine, but my tennis shoes were definitely more for fashion than hiking, and I got a huge blister on the back of my heel. But we'd already come so far, and I wanted to see the top. Like, if I'm going to have a blister, I'm also going to have the view.

We came to a scenic spot, and I looked around, and it was gorgeous. Breathtaking, actually. There were rocks jutting out over the side of a crazy-steep cliff over which you could dangle your feet and take in the scenery. It felt like we were a million miles up. Everything below us was small and covered with a thin layer of wispy cloud.

"Gosh," I sighed. "That's incredible. I'm so glad we took this hike. I'm so glad we made it to the top."

And I turned and Caleb was kind of giving me this look like...*Huh?*

"Babe," he said, pointing to a trail map post. "This isn't the top. We're only halfway up this mountain."

I'll spare you the swearing that ensued. I had come so far, in so much pain. How could I be expected to go any farther?

(PS: Caleb and I switched socks and I eventually made it to the top. PPS: Yes, that's kind of gross, but we have three kids—we've shared a lot more than feet sweat.)

I had stopped at a clearing on the trail up and mistaken it for the top of the mountain. That's sort of what happened after my breakup with Chris. I thought I was finished with the secrets in my life. I thought I was finished destroying myself. But I was only halfway there.

When I graduated from college, I didn't have anywhere to go. My plans had been smashed all to hell, and I was completely untethered. Geez, it was a Herculean feat just to *finish* college.

I moved back home and decided to get a temporary job as a secretary. At this point, I was trying to rebuild. Not even my life—just rebuild something.

And then I met a guy. Of course, right? Another man in my life would surely help the situation. I'd let the last man carve me out until I was a shell, so what was another one? My self-worth was nonexistent. If anyone had found out the truth about me, they wouldn't love me, anyway. I sure as hell didn't love me.

And this is when my rebellion *really* started to gain momentum.

Want to know who I chose? A closet alcoholic named Paul. Yup. Not that I have always managed my alcohol intake responsibly, but this guy drank every single day. He would show up to work reeking of booze. We didn't have sex, but we did hook up, because, like, now that I was damaged goods, what did it matter?

I didn't know he was a drunk at first. He had a doctorate in a medical field, which I thought meant he was a catch, and worked at the same place I did. Then one day, my boss pulled me into his office. He asked, "Um, have you seen Paul? He didn't come to work today. We're kind of concerned."

But come to think of it, I hadn't heard from Paul in over a

day. Turns out, they had to call the police. Paul was passed out drunk in his apartment, unconscious.

You'd think that would have taught me a lesson about drinking, but it didn't.

It did, however, cause me to end things with Paul. But it's not like I moved on to anything better. As it turns out, I was pretty good at partying. I could stay up later than anyone, because I didn't want to miss out on any of the fun. Maybe I was reliving the college days stolen by my relationship with Chris? There is no shortage of reasons why I was behaving the way I was.

Being the good girl definitely had not worked out for me. It was time to see how being the bad girl felt.

I stopped coming home at a decent hour. And sometimes, I didn't come home at all. My parents didn't know where I was, but I'm sure they knew that wherever it was, it couldn't be good. But they didn't know how to talk to me about it—I was their adult daughter who had come back from college.

They knew if they pushed too hard, I would just bolt. Like, I know I'm living in your house, but I'll be out on the streets before I let you tell me I have to be home at 10:00 p.m.

That's how I spent the entire summer. Just bouncing around and doing whatever I wanted to do, with no regard to what my parents wanted. God wasn't even in the equation anymore. It was a complete mess. I was a complete mess.

One night, my parents just sat me down. They were both pretty angry, because the night before I had strolled in around five o'clock in the morning.

"Where were you?" my mom asked.

I probably made up a lie or avoided the question altogether.

I wanted to be like, "Look. You don't want to know. Don't ask me questions, and I won't tell you any lies, okay? Just let me self-destruct in peace, would you?"

But my parents weren't having it. They basically begged me. "Kelsey, please tell us what's going on with you. We don't even recognize you, baby. Why are you living like this? This isn't who you are."

I told them I was trying to find myself. That I was figuring life out as I went. And basically, for them to mind their own business. They were devastated.

But, again, once I make up my mind, I'm going to do what I want to do. (Don't we all do that at some point? Some with more subtlety than others.) And I'm still like this, to a certain degree, but I have learned over the years that there's more than one way to learn a lesson.

See, I tend to be the kind of person who says, "Life's too short for regrets. Every bad choice I've made has taught me something. You gotta pick yourself up and move on."

But I'll be honest, thinking back to this phase of my life definitely challenges me in that statement. Coming out of it all and healing little by little over all these years has been a process.

And several years ago, when I was still in the thick of the healing journey, I probably would've told you I had all kinds of regrets. I would've changed it all if I could've gone back and done it over again.

Where I stand today, I still wouldn't necessarily say I have regrets (because I really do believe life is too short to live there). But I can also say with confidence that I wouldn't be who I am now had it not been for those handful of incredibly dark years that taught me invaluable lessons about who I am and whose I am. At this point in time, I wouldn't go back and change it, because I see the value of living through the dark phases of my life and how much more I appreciate the light once I walked back into it.

Well, yeah. But I could have learned most of those lessons without the regret. I could have learned them through wisdom—through listening to others or maybe even cracking open the Bible. I know, right? Novel idea. (I'm rolling my eyes at myself, here.)

You've probably heard this verse before, but it puts it about as simply as it gets:

"Trust in the Lord with all your heart. Do not depend on your own understanding. In all your ways obey him. Then he will make your paths smooth and straight" (Proverbs 3:5–6).

The NIV translation says, "Lean not on your own understanding."

In other words, you don't always know what's best for you. Don't put the weight of your life on your own understanding. If you do, you may end up lost down a deserted highway and not even know how you got there.

And me? I was doing a giant belly flop on my

> "Trust in the Lord with all your heart. Do not depend on your own understanding. In all your ways obey him. Then he will make your paths smooth and straight" (Proverbs 3:5–6).

understanding. When it came to making decisions, I was basically like, "That sounds good to me, so I'm going to do it."

My paths were anything but smooth and straight. They were crooked. They were winding. They were bumpy. My paths made no sense. But instead of listening to my parents, my God-given authority, I kept leaning hard on my own understanding.

It was this stubbornness—this unwillingness to reveal any of my secrets—that compounded the problems I was already grappling with. And I would definitely live to regret it.

Chapter 17

NASHVILLE BOUND

I grew up listening mostly to Christian music. It's just what was always playing. I was into bands like Avalon, Third Day, and Mercy Me. I especially loved Rachael Lampa. She signed her record deal when she was fourteen—*fourteen!* And when you hear her early singles, you think, *That's a grown woman.* But nope. She was barely a teenager.

I wore *out* her album *Kaleidoscope*. Like, it was a straight banger back in the early 2000s, and I would drive down the road and sing "No Greater Love" at the top of my lungs, all emotional and angsty when I was in high school. One time, I got to do a gang vocal with her in Nashville. (A gang vocal is basically a bunch of artists simultaneously recording together on a track.) I lost my mind over it and had zero chill.

In fact, one of my first "rebellions" as a teenager was branching out musically and listening to secular music. I hate that word, by the way—*secular*. It just sounds so negative when all it really means is not exclusively (or overtly) related to faith. I remember listening to country music in the car and feeling like such a badass. Like, *Hey, world, this song has NOTHING to do with God. What do you think of me now?* So dumb. Country music is as clean as it gets.

Then I really got naughty. I listened to Rihanna. I remember the very first time I heard one of her songs, and I immediately felt guilty for liking it. I literally had to pump myself up to listen to her. Like, *It's music, Kelsey. You're not a bad human for liking a song about an umbrella.*

I guess when I dreamed of moving to Nashville and becoming a singer, I imagined myself having stories like some of my favorite bands and artists. Like Katy Perry (who I actually got to meet backstage after her concert a few years back—yes, I cried like a super fan-girl, don't judge me). She started out as a Christian singer. Her first release was a gospel album, but when the label went belly-up, Katy went out to California and signed a new deal within like fifteen minutes.

Now, I'm not saying I ever thought I'd make it to her level—I didn't. I didn't even really want that, if I'm being totally honest. It's just that her career seemed to develop organically. Naturally. Beautifully. And that's not at all what happened for me.

So back to the summer before I moved to Nashville. I was still living at home and raising hell and terrifying my parents when a local radio station called me. I had a little hometown notoriety as someone who sang in college, so it wasn't any secret that I had a voice on me.

"Hey, Kelsey. We heard about this opportunity in Nashville with a talent management company. They're launching an all-girls Christian singing group, and they've reached out to us asking if we know anyone who would fit the bill. We immediately thought of you. What do you think?"

I had to smack my hand over my face to keep from laughing. *An all-girls group? A Christian all-girls group?* It sounded to me like the actual worst. Like, truly there was nothing I would have rather done *less* at that time in my life. I was in complete emotional and spiritual disarray. I had no desire to stand on stage with a bunch of other women to sing bubblegum Christian songs that I would definitely hate.

I immediately turned them down. I mean, I was nice about it. I thanked them for the opportunity and told them how flattered I was, and then I hung up. I knew I was *not* in a place in my life where I could successfully pull off whatever it was they wanted from me.

But they didn't leave me alone. They were like a jilted lover—no lie. They wouldn't drop it.

"Are you sure you won't consider it?" they asked again.

I sure hope I masked my annoyance. "No. It's really just not the right timing. But thank you."

"Okay," the lady barreled on. "Well, we're just going to send the form over your way. Just read it over, you know. And at least we'll be able to tell this management company that we did our part."

I got the form over email and it sat on the desktop of my computer, unopened, for weeks. And these people *would not leave me alone* about it. They kept reaching out like, "Hey, did you get a chance to look over the form we sent? Any chance you've reconsidered the opportunity?"

I kept saying no. No, no, no.

But when an opportunity keeps popping up, a wiser person might stop and think, *Hmm. I wonder why this keeps happening. I wonder if God is doing something. Maybe I should pause and actually consider what I might be missing here.*

Not me! At least, not then, I continued to just lean, lean, and lean on my own understanding.

One day I was at church with my parents, probably miserable as all get-out. And I looked around me. I realized that nothing had really changed about the place since I'd left and come back. The same people. The same songs. The same sermons. Even the fake floral arrangement in the lobby was the same. Everything was the same.

Only, I was different.

This can't be my life, I thought. *This cannot be where I end up. I cannot stay here. I have to get out. My future can't be leading me to stay where I am right now.*

Then the form popped into my mind. My ticket to a new life was sitting on the desktop of my computer. And I thought, *What the heck? I have nothing to lose. Like, I literally have nothing to lose. I may as well just fill out the stupid thing and see what happens.*

I went home and filled out the form, thinking nothing would probably come of it, and the very next day my phone rang. It was the CEO of the management company, and he said, "Kelsey, I read over your form. I watched the video you sent in. I was wondering if you'd be willing to come to Nashville in a few weeks for an actual, formal week-long audition. There's going to be lots of other girls. We've done a search nationwide and we want you to come. Would you come?"

And I said, "Sure. Yeah, I'll be there. What are the dates? Gives me the dates." I pretended to write them down and got off the phone.

I hung up, and my mom asked who I'd been talking to. I told her and she said, "Kelsey, what a huge opportunity!"

I probably rolled my eyes when she wasn't looking. "No, I'm not gonna go." I had sent the form in on a whim. An emotional reaction. I had already decided I didn't want to do it anymore.

She turned around. "But, Kelsey. You just told the man you'd be there."

And I was like, "Um, yeah. Yes ma'am, I did. But I'm not going to go. I just don't think it's what I want to do."

And because my mom will always be my mom no matter how old I am, when she gave me *the look*—you know the one— I knew whatever was coming next was going to be some type of strict instruction.

"Kelsey, if you're not going to show up for that audition, you *will* call that man and tell him you're not coming."

"But, Mom—"

"Kels! You want to be known as someone who keeps your word." Then she settled down a little. "Why don't you just think about it—just think about the audition."

So I went. Basically because I didn't want to make that call to the CEO. And also, because my parents kept drilling me that I would always wonder what could've been if I didn't try.

Have you ever seen an episode of *Making the Band*? That's what this experience was like—only, the faith-based version. They filmed everything from the moment we showed up to auditions. There were girls everywhere—I mean, so many girls. And we all took turns singing alone and singing with each other. And you guys—there were also *dance auditions*. Like, actual dancing while singing Britney Spears style—only think, more girls, more clothes, and no pythons. There's still footage of it all somewhere, but I can't bring myself to dig it up.

You see where this is going, right? Yep, I made the group. As soon as I was told, I was given ten minutes to call family and tell them before I was whisked away to have my virgin blond hair dyed red. Why? Because they already had a blonde and they needed a redhead. And I guess I looked like the weak and vulnerable link they could convince to do it. And they were right because a couple hours later, I looked like Ginger Spice. This is not a joke.

From day one in this group, I felt inadequate. Like, I wasn't *exactly* what they wanted, but I could sing, so I'd do, as long as they could change what I looked like. Dress me up like the red-haired Barbie part they needed me to play.

In all fairness, they asked me before dying my hair *but*…I also knew I didn't really have a choice.

Once again, I had to change something about me to please other people. I didn't exactly have a big, bright future ahead of me before this group, so I again gave up control of my own life. So, I let them dye my hair, chop it off, and move me into a house in Nashville with four other girls who were complete strangers to me.

None of us knew each other—we were all from different states. I tried to see the bright side. *This is your chance, Kels. Your new, fresh start. You're in a new city. No one knows you here. You can erase your past and be whoever you want to be.*

No one knew my backstory. They didn't know about Chris. And they would never even *guess* at my secret. I could rewrite my life in Nashville. Besides, isn't that what I'd always wanted?

The main problem with thinking we can escape our secrets is that we can't. (And yes, I laughed when I wrote that.) Honestly, we fool ourselves all the time. We tell ourselves, *If I can just behave for this amount of time, that part of my life will cease to exist.* But it doesn't. Unless we confront our stuff and call it out and share it with God, share it with someone else, and acknowledge it within ourselves. Otherwise, we just drag it around with us like a bag of dead bodies slung over our shoulder.

My parents always say that the day they dropped me off at that house, they both knew I was still so broken. When they pulled out of the driveway and waved through tears at me standing alone in the front yard, waving back with tears streaming down my face too, my mom said, "Your daddy and I were torn. We knew you were not okay. We knew you needed help. But we didn't know how to do that for you anymore. We didn't know how to reach you—how to find you. You were so gone. So lost. We had tried so hard. But we had to let you go. We had to let you find yourself."

My fresh start tanked pretty quickly. I had only been at the house a few weeks when I fell into the wrong crowd. Up until that point, I hadn't experimented with alcohol. But then I'd go out with all of these people who seemingly loved God so much (like, they were Christian artists for a living), and I saw that they drank, and it wasn't a big deal. It was just something that everybody in Nashville did. And, you know, since I'm an Enneagram seven, I didn't want to just sit idly by while other people experienced something fun. That just wasn't going to fly.

So, I started drinking. And I realized that drinking helped. It made things feel better. It made things feel numb. I loved it, actually. I loved the ability to escape. Alcohol and going out became something I did regularly. And by regularly, I mean basically every night of the week.

And…then I met a guy.

I could seriously throat punch myself for even having to tell you that. Because so far, I'd been garbage at choosing men. And shocker: This would be no different.

The guy I met was in the Christian music industry. Let's call this guy Jeremy the Grade-A Jerk (aka JTGAJ). JTGAJ and I started hanging out and talking, and one night, we were at this house party and they started pouring shots.

I had never done shots before, and I told JTGAJ. He was like, "How is that possible?" and he served me my first shot. Then my second. Then my third. Before the night was over, I had somewhere between ten and eleven shots. I can feel my throat closing up right now at the thought.

The next thing I remember is that I was throwing up in the bathroom—the one downstairs, right off the kitchen. I stumbled my way back to the den, and I must have passed out there. Then I have a vague memory of JTGAJ and his friend carrying me upstairs and putting me in a dark bedroom. That's my last memory of that evening.

I woke up several hours later—naked.

When I woke, it was still the middle of the night, 4:00 a.m. I grabbed my phone, disoriented but knowing I was in deep trouble. We had a curfew at the house. And I'd already missed it more than once. I'll never forget what I saw when I looked at the locked screen—twenty-six missed calls. Calls from my manager. Calls from the girls in the house. Calls from my parents. No one knew where I was.

When I woke up, I was alone in the bed. JTGAJ walked into the room shortly after with a pile of my clothes. "You should go home now," he mumbled, before turning and walking back out of the dark room.

And I thought to myself…Oh, Kelsey. You sure know how to pick 'em.

I sort of crawled out of the bed and started putting my clothes back on—not knowing what had happened to get them off in the first place. I was still drunk, so I'm sure half my buttons were missed and that I smelled like I'd taken a bath in a tub of vodka and vomit. To this day, I still don't have any recollection of what happened to me after I was taken upstairs. I can, of course, infer based on the state I was in when I woke up at 4:00 a.m.—but if I'm being honest, that unknown truth still haunts me sometimes and breaks my heart for that lost, desperate girl that night.

I am ashamed to say that I got in my car and drove myself back to the house. *Maybe I can sneak in. Maybe I can convince everyone this was a big misunderstanding.*

I had dried vomit all over me when I walked through the door. I took two steps inside before I realized they were all there—all four girls—sitting around the living room. Waiting for me. And they were not happy. I get it! It makes total sense. They were justified. They didn't know me. All they saw was a random, strange girl acting out. That I was wild. That I didn't come home at night. That I was blazing a mile-wide trail of destruction through the Nashville party scene, probably assuring our group's downfall before it even had the chance to start.

After that night, they told my manager that they wanted me out of the group. They told him about my drinking. About my staying out all night. About my apathy for the group and everything we were trying to do professionally.

My manager sat me down and had a come-to-Jesus talk with me. He told me the girls wanted to remove me from the group. He told me I had one last chance to figure myself out and settle down or I was done.

But knowing how the girls felt about me only made it worse. I never wanted to be at the house because I knew they didn't want me there. I was pissed at them. I thought of them as tattle-tales. So instead of partying less, I partied more. *No one's going to tell me how to live my life*, I thought. *Never again will I let someone control me.*

Chapter 18

HELP ME

On nights that I didn't have a party or bar to go to, I'd just drive the old country roads right outside of Nashville. Trying hard not to think and trying even harder not to feel. I felt like a spinning top at the end of its rotation. I had spun around and around and around. But the movement was slowing. The top was wobbling side to side. And soon, very soon, it was going to topple over.

He will make your paths straight.

I was still hungover from the night before the big storm and the phone call from my dad. Remember that night I described at the beginning of this book? I'd had another run-in with my manager. Another conversation. Another lecture. And this time, he'd apparently called my folks to tell them of my wild and destructive decisions.

A streak of lightning temporarily lit up the car as I drove in silence.

He will make your paths straight.

The thing I liked about the backroads of Nashville is that

they were *not* straight. They wound and curved and turned back in on themselves in certain places. I liked the unpredictability of it. I didn't want a straight path.

He will make your paths straight.

But the thing about a winding path is that you have to concentrate every single second. You have to be ready for anything. You have to know what's ahead.

He will make your paths straight.

I didn't know what was ahead. Not anymore. I couldn't see two inches in front of my face as far as my future was concerned. I was tired. I was empty. I was done. I had protected my secret. But I had left my heart completely vulnerable in the process, and it had been utterly decimated.

Then the rain started. Robotically, I turned on the windshield wipers. Now it was even *harder* to see what was in front of me.

And then I wondered, *What if I just drove my car into a tree? What if I just drove it off the side of a bridge? Would the pain stop then? Would I stop disappointing people? Would I stop disappointing myself?*

The phone rang—it was my daddy.

My dad, who had always stood in my corner, was one of the people yelling now too.

"We've been patient with you, Kelsey. We've tried to help you, baby, but we don't even know who you are anymore!"

Oh my God, I thought. *My daddy was my last chance. He was the last person on this planet who might still be able to rescue me if he found out the truth.* I tried to respond but instead I just sobbed because I knew this was rock bottom. I knew he was right. He didn't recognize me anymore, and honestly, I didn't recognize me anymore either.

It was something out of the twilight zone. Then he hung up.

The truth. I wasn't even sure what was true anymore. It had become so watered down. *I* had become so watered down in my pursuit of being what I thought everyone else wanted me— *needed* me—to be, I had stopped *being.*

Again, all I could pray was, *God—help me. Please help me.*

A bridge was up ahead. *This could be quick. I could end it all,* I thought. *I could finally escape all this hurt for everyone.*

I'm not even sure this happened consciously or because I made a willful decision to do it but, moments later, the tires of my car moved in the direction of the guardrail on the left side of the bridge—into the other lane. There were headlights in the distance. I knew if I kept going, I'd have to make a choice: Hit the car head-on or plunge off the side of the bridge.

Please help me.

There couldn't have been more than two minutes that passed between my dad's first phone call and his second phone call. It was that call that very likely saved my life in that moment. I snapped back to reality, jerked the wheel back into my lane to reach over and answer the phone again. But the second call may as well have been from a different person. When I picked up, his tone was instantly softer. He was actually sobbing. That made two of us. He was begging me—pleading with me.

"I'm so sorry I lost it. I'm so sorry I yelled. We're so just desperate. We love you so much, baby girl. We want to help you. Please let us help you."

The car that I had seen in the distance whizzed by me.

"Baby, baby, baby. I'm sorry. I'm sorry. I'm sorry. Help me," he said. "Help me help you. Help me help you, Kelsey. Let me be your daddy. Why won't you let me in?"

And I wanted to. I wanted to blurt out every single terrible thing that had happened to me. From growing up feeling trapped inside my own self—a girl who desperately wanted to be good, but also longed to know what she was missing out on. To getting to college and being told I wasn't good enough to sing there. To meeting Chris and being told I wasn't good enough to be his girl. To being abused. To moving home and feeling so disconnected from everything and everyone—especially God. To joining this girl group where I was obviously disappointing everyone around me.

I wanted to tell him everything. But I couldn't. I just couldn't. I didn't know where to start.

My dad told me to drive straight to my manager's house. So that's what I did.

"Kelsey, when I say this is your last chance," my manager said, "this is your *very last* chance."

I believed him.

"I've already called a friend and made you an appointment with him, so you can either show up at that counseling appointment tomorrow at eight a.m., or you can go home and pack your bags. His name is Rob, and he already knows you're coming. If you don't show up tomorrow, I'll find out. And I'll come to the house and pack you up myself."

Again, I believed him.

"So, what's your choice? Are you about done here? Do you want help? Or do you want to go home?"

I felt seen-through. I felt nothing. I felt everything.

"Help."

|||||||||||||||||||||||||

The day after my rainy car ride, I found myself sitting in a stranger's office, wondering how little I could tell him while still keeping my manager and parents happy. But that wasn't what happened.

Rob wasn't easily fooled. Nope. All my usual tricks of avoidance didn't stand a chance against his calm and direct demeanor. I would clam up. Stop talking. I'd talk about *anything* other than what was going on, and he'd just say, "We're going to talk about what matters most right now, Kelsey. And that doesn't matter most."

I was disarmed.

For the next few months, I spent hours upon hours in therapy on a brown leather couch, sitting across a small room from a man who would also save my life. It was like, once I started talking about it, I couldn't *stop* talking about it.

It being all I had been through. All I had felt—the pressure. The heavy hand of expectation at my throat for my entire life. I talked about everything except about what Chris did to me in the bedroom. Rob knew there was something. He just didn't know what.

At the end of one of our sessions, Rob leaned forward and he looked at me. "The next time you come in here," he said, "we're going to talk about you and Chris. And you're going to tell me what happened to you."

"You can't make me do that," I said, sounding *obviously mature and grown up.* "I can't tell you that, Rob. I just can't do it."

"You've got to start somewhere. Just tell me something. You don't have to tell me everything right away."

"I won't tell you."

"You'll tell me," Rob said. "You'll tell me, and you'll be okay. You can trust me, Kelsey. We'll get through this."

Well, damn.

I showed up the next week fully determined not to tell Rob. He couldn't make me do anything. No one could. Only, I found myself telling him everything.

"Tell me what happened," Rob said. "Start at the beginning."

As I talked about what Chris and I had done sexually, I couldn't make eye contact with him. I chose a spot on the floor to stare at and I didn't move my eyes from it and the truth fell from my lips like the raindrops had on my windshield the night I almost drove off the bridge.

I'll never forget that moment. It's like a snapshot in my mind that I can't erase, even if I wanted to. I felt so dirty. I felt so used. I felt so ashamed. And when I finished telling Rob about Chris, the room was quiet. So quiet, for so long in fact, that I finally forced my gaze from the floor. I looked up and Rob was sitting where he always sat across from me—but he had tears streaming down his face.

"First of all," he said, "I want you to know that I'm sorry that happened to you. I'm so sorry. Someone needs to tell you that. That they're sorry."

Wait, I thought. *Wait a minute. Shouldn't I be the one apologizing? Wasn't I the one who messed up?*

The next few paragraphs need a trigger warning for rape.

Then he continued with a handful of words that would change everything. "There's a term we use here in our world of counseling and therapy to describe what you've been through. And I want you to listen closely. It's a word you're not going to like to hear, but it's the correct term. It's called rape, Kelsey. That man manipulated you, controlled you, coerced you, and physically pushed you to do what he wanted you to do for him sexually against what you were comfortable offering. That's called rape. For nine long months, the man who claimed to love you—the man who asked you to marry him—raped you."

I started in quickly, "No, you don't understand—I didn't fight him, I didn't yell at him. I didn't even tell him no after a while—I, I…"

He interrupted me, "No, Kelsey, *you* don't understand. Any time a person is taken advantage of, and told things like, 'stop fighting it—it'll hurt less'—that's coercion and you were clear if he had to ask you 'stop fighting it and relax.' It was obvious you didn't want what he was pushing on you. It was obvious you were being hurt. You didn't ask for it. It was not consensual. And you need to see that as rape. You think it's your fault, don't you? It's not. That man had control over you. He manipulated you. He had a hold over you. And even if you wanted to get out—at *that* time—you couldn't have. And I'll spend the next six weeks, six months, six years—as long as it takes—until you start to believe and accept that.

"This is not something you chose, Kelsey," he continued. "You didn't bring it upon yourself. You didn't ask for it. You didn't even give consent. You were coerced and taken advantage of, and that's how I define rape."

With the realization of what had been done to me, my life was changed forever.

I want to stop and make a statement here about the most important part of my counselor helping me see what Chris did as rape. It finally made me accept that what had happened to me was something that was forced upon me for which I was not responsible. I believe rape is the right word when someone is sexually victimized. It shouldn't be seen as a one-size-fits-all experience. It's not only rape if a stranger man jumps a girl in a dark alley. It's not just rape if a guy breaks into a girl's bedroom at night and holds her at gunpoint and pushes himself on her. It's not only rape if drugs are slipped into a drink and the person is taken advantage of unconsciously. It's not only rape if it can end up in a courtroom. Rape can look like all kinds of unwanted, unconsented sexual advances. It's not always what we're fed on TV, in movies, or what we read. The point I'm making is that there are so many stigmas that surround rape and what constitutes rape or what it looks like. It's different for every sexually victimized individual.

So for you that are reading this, please hear me say...

If you've ever hooked up in any way because you felt like you had to for any reason, it's not your fault.

If you've ever gone farther than you wanted to because you felt like you had no other choice, it's not your fault.

If you've ever endured harassment, teasing, or flirtation because you knew if you said anything it wouldn't be taken seriously, it's not your fault.

Or if you stayed silent because you thought you'd be the one in trouble, it's not your fault.

It's *not* your fault.

You're *not* being dramatic or seeking attention if you tell the truth.

You *can't* find healing alone.

But there *are* people who can help.

Rob and I did a lot of work over the next several weeks. The time came to tell my parents, and again I dug my heels into the ground, refusing to do it.

Again, Rob was calm. "You told me. And you'll tell them, because they deserve to know. They've been involved in this process the whole time. All they want to do is love you. I know enough about your parents from listening to you talk about them. They adore you. They love you. They're here for you. They're standing in your corner. Give them the chance you never offered them, to love you through this. Let them be your parents."

And I was like, "Well, I'll call my mom and I can tell her, but I promise you, I will *never* tell my daddy. I can't."

Rob listened. But he told me I was wrong. He pushed. "Okay, but you will." That's just how he spoke to me. Not rude. Not condescending. Just quiet, direct truth.

I drove back to the house that day, and I sat in my car outside in the front and called my mom. And I told her everything. I left out no detail. She wept in pain. She wept in disbelief at how deep and awful it really was. She always knew that my relationship with Chris was dangerous and dysfunctional, but never did she dream of what really *happened*. Of course, she blamed herself. We love to do that as parents. We love to own our children's pain. We love to be responsible for *everything*. Since when did we become so powerful? We give ourselves too much credit. My babies are still tiny, and I already do the same thing with them. Try to shield them from the big, bad world. But ultimately, I know I can't.

I told my mom that it wasn't her fault. And I could never blame her for what happened. I never wanted her to carry that. And then I asked something pretty big of her.

"I need you to do something for me. I need you to keep this from Daddy until I can tell him myself. Because one, it's my story to tell. And two, I'm not ready yet. I'll tell him when I'm ready. And Mama? I'm going to be okay. I really am."

For the first time in a long time, I believed myself when I said it.

It was four or five months before I was ready to tell my dad. Rob kept gently prodding me to do it. "Nothing you could ever do would change your relationship with your dad, Kelsey. This won't. He's not going to love you less; he's going to love you *more*. You're going to give him a chance to be there for you in a real way for the first time in years."

I flew home one weekend and finally felt like it was the right time. I sat my daddy down. "I need to tell you something. I can't look at you while I tell you, but I need you to listen while I try to get through this."

I told him everything Chris had done and that I was sorry I hadn't been able to tell him sooner. I finally told my dad my deepest, darkest secret. It was horrible. It was freeing. It was healing. My daddy was everything I needed him to be for me in that moment and more. It hadn't made him see me any differently—in fact it drew us even closer together. For the first time in so long—I was seen. I was known. All the way through. And still loved for it.

My younger brother, Tyler, had also been home that weekend. I'm not sure of the details, but somehow, he had overheard the conversation with my dad. He must've hardly slept that night because I woke up super early the next morning to find Tyler draped over me and my blankets, shoulders shaking, his sobs muffled by the comforter.

"Oh my gosh." I sat up. "Bubby, what's wrong? What's going on?"

He buried his face in the pillow beside me. He couldn't look at me.

"Tyler, what's wrong?"

"I didn't know, Kels," he said between sobs. "I didn't know. And I was there. I was with you guys so much of the time. And I didn't even know. I didn't see it. I'll never forgive myself."

First me, then my mom, then Tyler—we all wanted to be the one to blame for Chris's actions. Why is that? Why is it that when we're disappointed or sad, every single thing is our fault? Why do we have so much trouble assigning blame to the right people? This "I'm bad" mentality is so pervasive—so sneaky. It has many of us convinced that we can do nothing right.

Self-blame is one of the most toxic forms of emotional abuse. We sit as the judge and jury at our own inner trial—neither of which God gives us permission to do. In Romans 12:19, we hear that God wants to own justice. It says, "I am the God who judges people." As He should! He's the only one whose perception is accurate. He's the only one who knows people's hearts and motives. Since when did we become smart enough (read: godlike) to judge anyone—including ourselves?

Self-blame does no one any good. It paralyzes us—keeps us from healing. It keeps our relationships from healing. It holds those we love the most at arm's distance. It keeps us from doing better and being better the next time we're faced with a hard choice. We think, *Well, I'm already a terrible person, so what does it matter?*

And it's so baffling to me. We grow up hearing about a big, loving God, and we think that's true. We believe that. We'll even repeat that. We'll say, "Oh, God is good all the time, and all the time God is good," and then we'll walk around feeling like total scumbags for yelling at our kids before they go to school.

Here's what I think the problem is.

While we're told from the pulpit that God loves us, what we often see demonstrated in conservative culture is that that love is conditional.

Be good.

Be quiet.

Sit still.

Don't make a mess.

Don't BE a mess.

Hide, hide, hide. Hide all the bad. Only show the good. Because they're watching. Everyone's watching.

"Tyler," I said, "are you kidding me? I wouldn't have made it those first few months without you. You were there for me when no one else was. How could you think that? This isn't your fault, Bubby. This isn't your fault."

My youngest brother, Chad, was also home that weekend.

I told him, too, and was met with nearly the same reaction as Tyler's. In a matter of two days, everyone in my family knew my big, bad secret. And you know what? They didn't love me less because of it.

If anything, my honesty made them love me more.

Chapter 19

JOSHUA AND THE GASLIGHTERS

Have you seen that meme that asks what color the dress is? I think there's another one about shoes. But it's like, "What color is this dress? If you see it as gold and white, blah, blah, blah." Have you seen that one? If you haven't, it's basically just a picture of a dress that can be seen as different colors by different people using different screens.

It sounds stupid, but basically the dress is actually black and blue, not white and gold. But a lot of people see white and gold. Like, I've seen this meme, and there's no way you can convince me the dress is blue. You cannot. But it is.

I'm sure you've seen this before: The same picture that can be seen two different ways. And both ways are one hundred percent accurate. They are both true. What it all comes down to is our perception. And I'm sure if you were to ask Chris, he'd have a completely different perception about what happened between him and me.

A few days after Chris and I broke up, I gave back his ring and we didn't speak again for a while. Then, three months later, just before I moved back home, he called me.

"Can we meet?"

I wasn't crying every day anymore. My brother had gone back to staying at his apartment. I wasn't ready to put on a clinic for the emotionally healed, but I was living. I should have said no to Chris. I didn't have the distance or space from him yet to even fully process everything.

But do you think I said no? C'mon, you know me better than that by now. I said yes. (Hi, I'm Kelsey, and I'm a glutton for emotional punishment.)

"Kels," Chris said. "Do you ever wonder if we've made a mistake? Do you think we could ever fix things and be together again?" I was too shocked to know how to respond. I told him I hadn't thought much about any of it since I had moved because I was too afraid to let my mind go there again.

We texted a little following that meeting and it was just insane how quickly he got back under my skin. He just knew me so well—he knew how to talk to me and coax me to get what he wanted.

Then, the night before I was supposed to move back home to my parents, he convinced me to meet up again one last time. "Don't go," he said. "Don't move. Please, Kelsey. I'm asking you. Just stay here. Stay with me."

We ended up making out and the entire time all I could think was *What in the actual hell are you doing, Kelsey? Didn't you just escape this?*

There's a scripture (Proverbs 26:11) that basically likens a person who repeats their mistakes to a dog returning to eat its own vomit. I mean, it's disgusting, but that's exactly what was happening. I was tucking a napkin in my shirt and bellying up to the table of my past mistakes.

"Don't go," Chris urged.

"Where am I going to go?" I asked. "I can't, like, move in with you. This is crazy."

"We'll go to my parents'," he said. "We have jobs there, Kels. Let's go there and take the future that was given to us."

Can you say *freaking trigger*?

It was like someone slapped me across the face. "Wait, no. No, I can't. I won't." I got up and sprinted away.

Not really. But that would have been funny. Emotionally, though, I did. I sprinted away and didn't talk to him again until one night not long after I'd moved to Nashville. Again, I wasn't winning any awards for making great life choices, but I was at least putting one foot in front of the other toward my goal of becoming a recording artist.

One night, I was sitting at the house I lived in with the girls from the group and we were all in the living room watching TV. My phone rang—but it only rang once. I looked at the screen and saw it was Chris, and my heart did one of those hyperactive racing stunts that makes you instantly nauseous. So, because I'm a glutton for all things self-destructive at this point, I texted him.

Did you mean to call me?

He answered, No, sorry. That was a butt-dial. Hope you're doing well.

I was still nauseous. How do you butt-dial someone on your phone whose number isn't intentionally pulled up or near your recent calls history? I didn't believe him.

Then a good twenty minutes later, he texted again: I'm sorry, I can't lie to you. I actually did mean to call you, but I freaked out and hung up after it started ringing. I called to apologize.

This perked me up. This piqued my interest. This, I was here for. We started texting.

He had been following me through mutual friends (who had all sided with *him* in our breakup), and they knew that I was in Nashville and knew about the group. He told me he wanted to apologize but would rather do it in person or over the phone. So, I called him.

"I'm sorry," he said. "I want to own my part in what happened between us."

He didn't ever address the sexual part of our relationship. He kept his apology very general. It was a very Chris-esque thing. *I want to be the bigger person and let you know that I know I wasn't perfect.* I mean, it was kind of stupid, but at least he acknowledged that I wasn't some psycho, running away from a great thing.

We ended up talking for about three or four hours. And it's insane, but all those old feelings came rushing back to the surface. All the good times came to mind. All the stuff that "worked" in our relationship. (At this point, you may be thinking, *There were actually some good things about your relationship with Chris?*)

And we'd continue to text off and on for a couple weeks maybe. I was dipping my toe in yet again. Yeah. (Hi, I'm Kelsey, and I'm a moron sometimes.)

I didn't know the next part of this story until way later, but at the same time Chris had started to reach out to me for that "apology" (which prompted our texting again), my brother Tyler was still in college. (Keep in mind, this was months before my therapy breakthroughs with Rob or the point at which I told my family what happened.)

The fall after I graduated and moved to Nashville, Chris started to reach out to Tyler to hang out—watch football games, go to coffee—at the same time he had reached out to "apologize" and reignite our communication. And since Tyler didn't know the truth yet, they started to spend some time together. All the while, Chris was asking Ty all these questions about me and how I was doing. I think he was trying to regain access to me. Controlling the corners of my life because he couldn't control me anymore.

Manipulative, much?

On the phone that night in Nashville, Chris asked, "Do you ever think about what could have been? Do you ever think about us?"

Let me pause right here. Because I know all of you are wanting to reach through the page or screen you're reading this on and bang my head against the table a few times. And you're right—I was playing with fire. But we all do this to a certain degree, don't we? When it comes to the temptation to repeat past mistakes?

We send that text we know we shouldn't.

We say yes to another thing we know we should skip.

We click on that Instagram page even though we know how it makes us feel.

We snap at our loved ones even when we know we should be patient.

We don't seek God's wisdom when it's time to make a big decision.

I'm not one of those people who has hundreds of scriptures memorized. But I do remember one (probably for the wrong reasons). It always makes me laugh.

In Matthew 15:16 (NIV), the disciples are asking Jesus about a specific parable and what it means. I guess it irritated Jesus because He says, "Are you still so dull?"

Like, um, are you still this stupid? Are you still this naïve? Are you still doing the same dumb things over and over again and expecting a different result (which is, of course, the definition of insanity)?

There's a story in the book of Joshua that I think is so important (9:1–10:15). I can't lie, the books in the Bible on war and lineage get a little heavy for me, but we can learn so much about human nature and about the nature of God from reading them.

In this passage the Gibeonites had heard about all the victories Joshua and the people of Israel had been having in battle. They thought, *Obviously, Joshua is bad to the bone. Obviously, this is someone we want on our side.*

They didn't want Joshua to remove them from the Promised Land where they lived (as God had commanded him to do), so they came up with a plan. They loaded down their donkeys with old, cracked wineskins and they put their worn-out sandals on their feet. They dressed in their old, ratty clothes, and they even took moldy bread with them.

As someone who can overexaggerate, I really have to hand it to the Gibeonites for committing to their ruse. But I don't know if even I could hang with people who eat rotten food just to get what they want.

Anyway, imagine standing there as you see the Gibeonites approach with the look of exhaustion and hunger. Picture their threadbare clothing and patched sandals. Their cracked wine-skins and old bread. I mean, think about how it all probably *smelled*.

Now, as people who love God, put yourself in Joshua's shoes. When the Gibeonites claim to be from a distant land seeking peace, what's your first move? You make peace. They're hungry! They're poor! But Joshua had a command from God *not to* make peace with anyone from outside the Promised Land.

Think about it. Every input to your senses is feeding your brain, telling you that they are being honest. Their story matches the evidence given.

What do you do?

Well, Joshua did what *felt* right. Sure, he asked them a few questions, but in the end, he made a peace treaty with the very people God had told him not to make peace with.

This wasn't the first time Joshua rolled like this. In the beginning of chapter 6, Joshua went to God on how to take Jericho. As you probably remember, God told Joshua how to win in a way that would prove that it was only God's hand in the victory. But then, in the very next battle at Ai, Joshua didn't go to God. He made his own plans, and the Israelites were whooped.

Joshua knew better than to do his own thing. He knew better than to disobey God. But he did it anyway. And when he found out that the Gibeonites were actually his neighbors in the Promised Land, everybody in the community got up in a tizzy with him.

It's not shocking, right? That we can make the same mistake twice? That we can believe someone who is deceiving us? But we play a part in that deception when we do things we know better than to do. Fool me once, shame on you...you know the rest.

And I knew better than to talk to Chris. To even crack open that dark door. Yes, the evidence all pointed to the possibility that maybe he'd changed. He'd apologized, after all. But could I trust him?

Should I trust him?

Chapter 20

WHEN GOD SPRINTS TOWARD YOU

Thankfully, before I could do anything truly stupid with Chris, one day I just…snapped out of it. (Again, I'm sure the Holy Spirit gave me a loving but firm nudge that I probably wasn't aware of at the time.) I remembered why I'd gotten out in the first place and sent a short but sweet "we're done here" text and never looked back. But damn, that was close.

Later on, I found out that my dad sent Chris an email. Though I never read it, I'm pretty sure the threats in that email were not veiled at all. I'm pretty sure the message in that email was very, very clear.

If I ever hear that you've gone *anywhere near Kelsey OR Tyler*, I will [fill in the blank with something violent and menacing]. You've done nothing but cause our family pain. And I *KNOW* what you did to my daughter, Chris. I know *everything*.

But seriously, though. Why did I almost make the same mistake *again*?

Regardless of the "evidence," I knew with a deep-down conviction that Chris was bad for me. The entire time we'd been talking, he'd been seeing another girl in Nashville and making trips back and forth to visit her. Honestly, it would be pretty hard to convince me he wasn't looking for an opportunity to run into me.

I was sure Chris wasn't finished being manipulative. And he hadn't changed at all.

But thankfully, I had.

|||||||||||||||||||||||

Before I wanted to be a professional singer, if you would've asked me what I wanted to be when I grew up, I would have told you a scuba diver. Which literally makes me laugh out loud because as an actual grown-up, I'm absolutely terrified of all things fish and ocean.

We recently went to Panama City Beach, Florida, on vacation with my family. I love Panama City, by the way. I think it gets a bad rep because so many parents today went there for spring break and have regret tattoos and bad memories from it. But it's not all a bad place.

My mom is always trying to get me to get into the ocean, and I was like, "No way. No freaking way." But my kids were watching, and I don't want to give them ocean wounds, so I got in all the way up to my waist. So…where's my gold star?

Anyway, I was feeling pretty proud of myself and for a minute there, I thought, *Maybe I could be an ocean person. This isn't so bad. This is…*

Then something brushed my leg. I flipped. I was screaming, "Shark! Shark! Shark!" as I high-kneed it back to the safety of the good old fishless shore. When I finally got out, I realized that everybody around us was looking at me. They were like, "Who is this crazy woman? Somebody take that lady's Yeti away. Cut her off!"

Nope. I was sober. I was just *that* terrified of the ocean and what lives in it. I think I'd rather be just about anything *other* than a scuba diver.

Anyway, while we were there, a hurricane landed on shore and the weather was indescribable. The wind was just insane. You could hardly step outside without being blown side to side. The condo we were staying in had a balcony from which we watched the storm roll in, and it was *not* happy with the elements. It groaned and creaked, and at one point I thought, *Is this thing going to implode on us now?*

But there was also something beautiful about the storm. About the way the sky looked, layered in angry grays, hovering over an agitated ocean.

The thing is, I like storms. I like watching them. I like hearing them. I like tracking them on apps and seeing which weather person's predictions are right or wrong. #SignsThatYou'reOld, amiright?

Chris may have brought the storm to me, but I brought that storm with me to Nashville.

The girl group I was in put out a record. I was in counseling, I had stopped partying, and I had no further communication with Chris. But still—it felt like I'd never be whole again. Maybe my family loved and accepted me again. But they were my family—they had no choice. But what about God? What about this God I'd grown up loving and wanting a relationship with?

It sounds weird, but I felt shy toward God. I felt like I wanted to hide my face from Him.

Probably one of the first Bible stories ever taught to me was the one about the Prodigal Son. I grew up thinking that the Prodigal Son was an idiot and that it was the older brother who was the real MVP. That was probably because when I heard it the first few times, I *was* the older brother. But when I heard the story as an adult, it hit differently.

Right after I moved to Nashville, I stumbled onto this giant church downtown. It was just like a cool place. All the single people went there, and it was all vibey and loud and everybody dressed well. It was *the place* to go to church.

I say that I stumbled into this church because I didn't want to be at church. I didn't even know at the time if I believed in God anymore. A friend invited me to go, and I agreed. Then I immediately regretted it. But I knew what it was like to invite someone to church and really want them to come, and I didn't want to disappoint my friend. I dragged my butt there—

probably still had the stamps on my hands from the bars the night prior.

Wouldn't you know it, but the message that night was on the Prodigal Son. The pastor taught about the older son, who did all the right things and who expected a reward in return for everything good that he'd done. *That used to be me*, I thought.

The other son just screwed around and was like, "Peace out, Dad. Just give me my money."

At that time, in that culture, asking for your inheritance early, before the death of your parents, was basically like saying, "You are dead to me, Dad. I don't care about you. I just want your money. I want my freedom. I want to leave, and I want to do whatever I want to do. I want to live my life the way I want to live my life."

I obviously resonated with that younger son, because I had recently felt all of those things. Like, verbatim.

I was now the younger brother. The prodigal.

The pastor went on to tell the story about how the father longed so deeply for his son to come back home. How it grieved his spirit to lose his youngest. How it broke his heart.

I wasn't a parent then, but I am now. And I can't imagine my daughter, Collins, coming to me and saying, "Hey, Mom. I actually don't respect you, and to be honest, I don't love you. You can make the check out to cash, because I'm out of here."

Here's what happened after the Prodigal Son left:

Then he left for a country far away. There he wasted his money on wild living. He spent everything he had. Then the whole country ran low on food. So the son didn't have what he needed. He went to work for someone who lived in that country. That person sent the son to the fields to feed the pigs. The son wanted to fill his stomach with the food the pigs were eating. But no one gave him anything. (Luke 15:13–16)

It's not shocking that the younger son blew through the money. I mean, the kind of person who does what he did by asking for his inheritance early is exactly the kind of person who would *not* be able to manage that inheritance very well.

The son eventually ran out of money, and he was probably like, "Crap. Even the pigs I feed are eating better than I am. This is what rock bottom looks like and I need help."

The son realizes this and then he has an idea. The New International Reader's Version translation says it this way: "Then he began to think clearly again." (Luke 15:17 NIRV)

Isn't that how it works? We mess up and we look around us at the destruction and the chaos—the consequences of our actions. And we're like, *Wait, what? What did I do? Who was that making all those stupid choices? Was that me? Did I do that? I've got to get out of this. I've got to go back home.*

So the Prodigal Son dusts himself off and gives his notice to the pig owners and he heads back to the father whom he'd betrayed. *I'll be one of his servants*, he told himself. *Even they live better than I've been living.*

Here's what happened next:

So he got up and went to his father. While the son was still a long way off, his father saw him. He was filled with tender love for his son. He ran to him. He threw his arms around him and kissed him. The son said to him, "Father, I have sinned against heaven and against you. I am no longer fit to be called your son." (Luke 15:20)

The pastor that night explained a critical part of this story I'd never heard before. Here's the thing about that reunion between the father and the son. In that culture, people didn't run. It was almost disrespectful. You don't run unless there's something wrong. It was a very noble culture; you walk. And not only that, but you walk with your head held high—you walk tall, and you walk slowly.

But the dad saw his son coming in the distance. And I just imagine how he must have felt. *Could that be...is that...is it him?*

The son was probably still half a mile away when the dad confirmed that it was his youngest son, way off in the distance, slowly walking the dirt road toward him. When he recognized it was him, the dad dropped what he was doing and he took off, sprinting recklessly toward his son as fast as his feet could carry him, his arms stretched wide open. The son—full of shame and regret—immediately started groveling.

"I'm worthy of nothing. I am a complete screwup. I am nothing. You don't even have to call me son anymore."

And the father says, "Son, you're home. You're here. I don't care where you've been or what you've done. I'm just so glad you're home. You have no idea how much I love you and how much I missed you. You have no idea how much I've cried for you."

This man, this father, he abandoned every cultural norm in that moment. Just out of pure instinct and unconditional, reckless love for his son, he took off sprinting toward him and forgave everything that the son had done to him. Miraculously, he took him back without any questions asked.

This pastor that night said, "That is how God feels about you. God pursues you so passionately, leaving nothing behind. Doesn't matter where you've been or what you've done—He just takes off running toward us because His love is so deep for us."

I remember sitting there and I was just sobbing. *If what he's saying is true—if He is this kind of God, the kind of God who would drop everything and come for me, the kind of God who would pursue someone like me to that extent, then I have to know who He is. I have to know.*

Something shifted in my heart that night. "Okay, God. You have my attention. If you're there, if you're really there and you're really not just here to make me live my life a certain way, and you're not going to condemn me for the things I've done and the things I'll do in the future, if you actually just love me for the broken human that I am right here, then I'm listening. I want to know you and I want you to show me who you are."

That was the beginning of my journey back to Jesus. And just like the father in the parable, He abandoned everything and came out running to meet me.

Chapter 21

WHEN YOUR GOOD IS GONE

You wanna know what word I hate? Actually, there are a lot of words I hate. Let's make a list.

- Moist (like the rest of the world)
- Crusty (like it just implies something gross)
- Curd (rhymes with an even more disgusting word)
- Slacks (they're pants, Karen)
- Crevice (sounds crusty)
- Fetus (why not call this a teeny, tiny little baby?)
- Phlegm (honestly, it sounds exactly like what it is)

Do you have any words that you hate? Did I just add some to your list? Sorry about that, but those are like, vomity. Okay. Add *vomit* to the list, too. Blech.

There's actually a little science behind us hating certain

words. Linguist Jason Riggle and neuroscientist David Eagle-man believe that "word aversion comes from the sounds them-selves."[8] The vowel and the consonant combinations just sound off to our ears—kinda like when we hear an off-key note. The sounds made by the words we don't like sort of splinter in our ears.

One word I grew to hate was the word *forgiveness*. It's just tossed around so much—especially in the Christian world. It sounded watered-down to me for so many years. What did it really mean?

I needed forgiveness. I wanted forgiveness.

But I thought I could never fully be forgiven for what I'd done. I had no real concept of a God who could forgive me. And if He could forgive me, could I ever actually forgive myself?

After the church service where I heard the story of the Prod-igal Son, something was stirred inside of me. Something that I couldn't drink away, party away, or even explain to myself. I couldn't name it at the time, but now I believe it was the Holy Spirit.

When I was young, I wanted to walk with Jesus from the jump. I trusted in Him blindly and wildly. I wanted to be a part of His story. I mean, remember I'm an Enneagram seven. I want to be a part of *every* story. But God's story sounded espe-cially exciting. Somewhere along the way, though, what I wanted became unimportant. It became almost sinful. And my childlike faith became adult-like obedience.

Why was I stuck in such a cycle of shame and self-blame for so many years? Whose fault was it? It was no one's, in particular.

Not my pastor's. Not my church's. It was definitely *not* my parents' fault.

But when a culture's expectations can rob someone of the very thing it professes to give them, we have to start asking questions. Perhaps it's what we often hear about the difference between God-given faith and man-made religion. And as I said at the start of the book, I have no ax to grind with the Evangelical church. I do have a problem, however, with some of the unspoken rules that have invaded this glorious journey of following Jesus. Can you relate? Do you just get tired sometimes of the culture we've created? The unspoken expectations on how to look, or to be, or to do good? And that's just it: God didn't create our religious culture—we did.

But that night at the church something shifted for me. It was like all the guilt traps and triggers that made me doubt my worth (inside my head and from our culture) melted away, and all I could sense was the love of God. His Spirit was saying, *Come home, Kelsey. I'm here. I'm waiting. I'll run out to meet you. But you have to take the first step. Come back home.*

And I wanted to. I wanted to feel close to God again. But I'd never learned how. Look, maybe there were lessons on grace that I missed or didn't connect with growing up. Maybe I was sitting in the back of the room, talking during those messages. (This is actually likely.) But back then? I didn't think I needed the grace because of my "goodness." Because

> All the guilt traps and triggers...melted away, and all I could sense was the love of God.

my *good* was bigger than His *grace*. (Sounds arrogant now, but at the time, I felt nothing but proud.)

But when my good was gone?

I wanted to go *home*. But where was home? I couldn't return to the faith I'd known before, because what I understood of it was that it was conditional. It was based on behavior. It was counterfeit. Counterfeit because I'd always accepted it at face value—I'd never made it real. Made it mine. Yes, in my experience, Christian culture gave me mixed signals. But I shoulder the weight of never taking the time to sit down with the Bible to get to know God for myself.

It takes work. Although work was something I'd always been good at. When I was in high school, a family friend was the manager of the Ace Hardware around the corner from my house. He hired me to work there, and I *loved* it. My friends would come visit me, and I would totally try to impress guys with my knowledge of ratchets and weed whackers.

In college, I sang for money—scholarship money. Then I worked at Chris's parents' church. Afterward, I was in the girls' group. But we didn't actually get paid. Not yet. We were given a house and small monthly stipend, but it wasn't nearly enough to even feed myself. I'll never forget the car I had when I moved to Nashville. Her name was Baby Blue, and she was a 1992 baby-blue Toyota Camry that looked like a nightmare but ran like a dream.

I had to get an actual job while we were recording, so I worked at a Starbucks in a local mall for the first year. I once sold a cup of coffee to Martina McBride. And then I moved to the Sunglass Hut in the same mall.

Okay, funny story. When I worked at Sunglass Hut, a super-famous R&B artist came into the store. I'm not going to name him here, because he's since been in a little legal trouble, but he was very, very well known, especially at the time.

So, my foray into edgy music pretty much began and ended with Rihanna, and I had no idea who this guy was. There had been a couple of people in the store, and I noticed that my manager was slowly shuffling them out. I didn't think much of it. I was at the register, and this musician walked in with his bodyguard. Then they shut the store doors and locked them. I was like, *That's weird*, but I didn't care, because I mean, I wasn't planning on making a career there or anything.

So he walked over and he knew exactly what he wanted. He picked up a pair of Versace sunglasses and brought them to the register, and I acted completely normal. Because I *still* didn't realize the guy was an international celebrity. Granted, he did already have a pair of sunglasses on. I just thought the guy might be kind of douchey.

At the end of our spiel to guests, we're supposed to get their contact information. So, I rang him up, took his card, and went to enter his information.

"Can I get your phone number, please?" I asked.

Behind him, my manager whipped around and gave me the *NO! STOP!* look. I said, "Um, or not?" *Great job at not making it awkward, Kels.*

The guy sort of looked around, like, *Are you kidding me?* I said, "Have a great day," and handed him his bag, still totally clueless.

I was so embarrassed. But also, he could have just said, "No, thank you." He had definitely been irritated at me. When I left the mall that day, he was sitting on a bench outside, surrounded by his spoils from the shopping trip and fans trying to take pictures. I just walked right on by.

I've given voice and piano lessons. I've worked as a server (shoutout to Texas Roadhouse and their honey butter—that was one of the best jobs I've ever had). I've done whatever it took to make ends meet. I'm no stranger to hard work.

But I'd never put in the work when it came to my faith—when it came to getting to know God. When it came to reconciling with Him and forgiving Chris for what he did to me and forgiving myself for what *I* did to me.

I have to be honest—forgiving Chris would have never happened had I not come clean to my parents. So, if I were the type of person who was going to give you a numbered list (which would never happen because I hate lists), that would be the first thing I'd say I had to do: forgive this man who had wounded me and abused me in so many ways.

In order to forgive someone, we first have to be honest about what was done to us. We have to tell someone else. Get the secret out—loosen its power over us. And if it's not a secret, we need to get the truth out. What actually happened? Which parts can I own, and which parts was the other person responsible for?

I told people that I trusted. I told Rob, my counselor, and then I told my parents.

If you've never tried therapy, you are missing out. I have been in and out of therapy of all sorts since meeting Rob. Rob is still a friend of ours—he did our premarital counseling. I think back in the day, therapy was probably frowned upon by a lot of people in the circles I ran in. But now? At this point in the twenty-first century, I think there is much less of a stigma in the church toward counseling.

Therapy (or counseling) used to be seen as something that only *super*-messed-up people found themselves in (but, real talk: Aren't we all messed up?). Now I think most Christians see it as an often vital part of our individual journeys toward wholeness. I can say with complete conviction that I would not be where I am today—or who I am today—without the help of a professional counselor.

I don't know who needs to hear this, but get you some help!

If you're reading this and you've been deeply hurt, assaulted, or abused, I know you may never get the chance (or want the chance) to face the person who hurt you. Maybe it wasn't even a person—maybe it was a company or a culture. That's okay. Write them a letter and then throw it into a fire or something. (Safely.) Get straight old-school youth group with it. There's so much value in telling a person they've wronged you, even if you don't get to tell them personally.

Finally—and this is the hardest part—time helped. The passing of time, and the constant letting go. I realized that my unforgiveness toward Chris only tied me to him. And that's the last thing I wanted. But the obsessing over the awful things he'd done to me kept him and our relationship at the forefront of my mind. I knew that if I wanted to move on and find joy again, I had to let him go—let my unforgiveness go.

No, what he did was not okay. It was vile and it was gross. But my unforgiveness was hurting me a whole lot more than it was hurting him.

If I wanted to move on and find joy again, I had to...let my unforgiveness go.

Chapter 22

GRACE > REGRET

Trauma is a tricky thing.

And if you've been through anything like I went through, you most certainly have been traumatized. And yes, PTSD can be a part of it. The key thing I can say here—again—is *get help*. Friends and family are a great place to start (your "safe circle"), but the deep waters of trauma sometimes require a trained professional therapist to help us escape the undertow.

I'll be honest. Some days, I still wake up hating Chris's guts. My marriage and my sex life will forever have traces of the trauma in them because I am a human being. I can forgive, but I can't forget. I pray to forget—at least the worst, most terrible memories—but that's the Holy Spirit's job. I trust God with that part of my journey—to heal my memories and allow me to "forget" in the sense of letting go of the pain.

Trust me. I've tried to forget the whole godawful nightmare. But in those moments—those moments where I feel the unforgiveness bubbling in my gut—I take a step back.

"I forgive him, God," I'll say, even though I feel the opposite. I remind myself that I am not my past. It doesn't define me, and it doesn't have a hold on me anymore. I am good enough and loved already.

After forgiving Chris, the other person I had to forgive was myself. Which took a little longer, ironically. I made a series of decisions that led me into the position to be abused. And then, instead of being honest about what had happened, I covered up my shame with lies, men, and booze, which only served to further injure me and stave off any kind of healing I hoped to experience.

I remember telling Rob once, "I should have known better. I should have done better. I can't forgive myself."

He just stared at me. "You mean you *won't* forgive yourself."

"I don't think I can," I said back.

"But aren't you tired?" he asked. "Tired of hating yourself so much?"

I was. I kept replaying the events of the last two years over and over in my mind like a merry-go-round, sickened by how far I had let everything go.

When I came back the next session, Rob gave me a list of scriptures. This was rare for him: He never hit me over the head with spirituality. He was subtle—basically sliding the handwritten card across the coffee table between us.

"If you have time," he said, nodding at the verses.

Well, the last thing I felt like doing was reading the Bible. But I knew I had to do something different if I wanted my life to change for the better. So, I looked them up.

"So if the Son of Man set you free, you will really be free" (John 8:36).

That was the first one. At first, I was like, *What the heck does this have to do with forgiving myself?* But then I thought about it a little deeper. We first have to recognize that our guilt and shame is only assigned to us by ourselves. We do that. We do that to others, and we do that to ourselves.

> "So if the Son of Man set you free, you will really be free" (John 8:36).

But Jesus doesn't condemn you. He didn't do that then, and He doesn't do that now. The mantle of "being bad" is something we shrug into. We come into this world and slip into an invisible river of comparison- and shame-based living, whether it's because of theology or bad habits or bad character. But our actions are separate from who we are in the eyes of God.

Who we really are? We are God's children. We are God's masterpiece. We are His final and ultimate act as Creator.

He sent His only Son to continue His relationship with us. To prove His love for us. Which was Rob's next verse: "But here is how God has shown his love for us. While we were still sinners, Christ died for us" (Romans 5:8).

Again, please see this: The cross wasn't an act to rescue hated, rejected orphans from a disgruntled and angry Father. Jesus didn't say, "Hey, God, look down there at earth…Who are all those terrible creatures you call your sons and daughters? I tell you what, I will go down there and in exchange for my sacrifice, they can become lovable to you again." No! Jesus' death and resurrection was a *transformational* victory that restored us to an already loving Father. Jesus didn't die and rise again so we could be loved; He endured the cross so we could be restored—forever, unconditionally.

In God's abundant love for each of us, He sent Christ to die for us. And by doing so, we would no longer be separated from Him by the darkness of our world. God never intended for us to get it all right. In fact, He knew we wouldn't get it right (*insert Christ*). Perfection is not a requirement. We weren't forgiven based on getting things right. So if God forgives us, why do we struggle with forgiving ourselves?

It's our humanity. It's our inability to forget what we've done. It's that record of our mistakes playing over and over until the needle scratches and it starts all over again. It starts when we enter this fallen, broken world—plusses and minuses, good deeds and bad deeds.

It's our trying to comprehend a love that we simply cannot comprehend. Like, how do you explain color to someone who has never seen mauve, aqua, or sienna red before? We don't have the ability, the language, the capability to even approach the complexity and depth of the love God has for us.

The second way I forgave myself was to study all the ways God demonstrated His love for me—for His people.

So, if Jesus' death on the cross

> So if God forgives us, why do we struggle with forgiving ourselves?

was enough to prove His radical love for the whole world, who the heck are we to say that our sin is so bad? Our sin is so different? That our sin is so special? We look at our neighbor's Instagram and we're like, *She's posting AGAIN about her devotional time? Is she ever NOT praying? Why does her house look so clean? From how DOC looks like a Christian.*

We tend to put sin on different levels. A small white lie isn't as bad as constantly lying, right? In God's economy, it's all the same.

"Suppose you keep the whole law but trip over just one part of it. Then you are guilty of breaking all of it" (James 2:10).

It's like, either you're perfect or you're not. And none of us is perfect. Duh. I've probably messed up ten times in the writing of this book. But you're no better *and* no worse than your super-spiritual neighbor. God loves you both the same, and He looks at you both the same.

This is probably going to get me in trouble, but that's really never stopped me from doing or saying things before. So…

That person who hurt you. God loves you both the same, and He looks at you both the same.

That politician who makes your teeth grind. God loves you both the same, and He looks at you both the same.

God's love is immense. His forgiveness even more so. And He offers it to everyone, equally, all the time, no matter what. And we hear that, and we say, "Yeah, that's true for other people. But not me. You don't know what I've been through. You don't know what I've done."

This kind of thinking is exactly what got me stuck. And it's the same exact thing as saying "I know more about me than God knows about me." Which is ridiculous.

For me in my present life, there is no scenario where this line of thinking gets me more caught up than in my parenting. Parent guilt is real, y'all. It's real.

When my oldest son, Emmett, was thirteen months old, my girlfriend and I took him and her baby to the park. It was January, but it had been a mild winter. I still put Emmett in these completely adorable boots with rubber soles. While we were playing, he asked if he could go down this wide metal slide. He was too small to go alone, so I put him on my lap and down we went.

Well, my slide game was apparently off that day, because we went rocketing down that sucker at the speed of light. Somewhere along the way, Emmett's boot caught the slide and twisted his little leg the wrong way. He started screaming the instant we got to the bottom of the slide. But honestly, it had all happened so fast that I didn't know yet what actually happened with his leg. I assumed the speed of the slide just scared him, and he was crying about that. When I started looking him over to see if anything was wrong, my friend told me she noticed his boot catch the edge of the slide coming down. Maybe the boot just twisted his leg and he was sore. But when I tried to put him down to stand on his own, he couldn't. His crying became inconsolable.

Cue panic.

I drove him to the pediatrician, and she sent us right to the ER. "I think it's broken," she told me. "Take him now."

I was pregnant with Beckett at the time, and I couldn't be with my sweet baby boy for any of his X-rays. I was literally doubled over in the hospital hallway in hysteria, hearing my baby scream through the closed door. When I say I was a wreck, I was like a ten-car pileup. Sure enough, it was broken, and Emmett was fitted for a cast.

I'll never forgive myself, I vowed. *Never.*

Sure enough, I tortured myself for a very long time to get over what happened to Emmett. I was heartbroken for him. I cried for days and days and days. And when it came time to tell the story of how he'd broken it, my shame grew.

I'm the mom, I would tell myself. *I'm the one who is supposed to protect him. Instead, I'm the reason he broke his leg.*

A day or two of tears would have probably been natural, right? No one wants to see their baby in a cast. It's pitiful. But I agonized, and I didn't sleep at night, and I felt so much guilt. Why? Because I was embarrassed? Because I wasn't the perfect mother?

It sounds laughable, but I think most moms feel this pressure—this pressure to be perfect. To be Instagram-worthy at all moments of the day. And it's perpetuated by our culture almost more than any other type of shaming I've personally ever experienced.

We're expected to have sparkling kids in matching outfits who behave perfectly and smile on cue. We're expected to feed them all-organic foods and manage their screen time with a stopwatch. We're expected to teach them Bible verses, plan playdates, and give them a Harvard-level education before they start kindergarten. *And we're supposed to do all of this while losing the baby weight and making time for self-care.*

Self-care? Like, what even is that? As I write this, I have three kids ages four and under. My self-care is the glass of wine I have after I finally wrestle them all to bed. My self-care is a work-out video in the playroom with at least two of my kids hanging off my limbs. But I see posts from all these moms who journal, and have nighttime skincare routines, and go on hikes with their girlfriends.

I feel like I should have it all and do it all and be it all as a mother. The only problem with that is that it's impossible. The truth of it all is that motherhood (and parenting in general) is messy. It's not pretty or glamorous. It's so much trial and error and just taking it a day at a time. Lowering your unrealistic expectations of both yourself and your kids.

And give yourself tons of grace when stuff just happens on your watch that sicks you out—like the time I was trying to nurse a screaming, hungry baby for a quick five minutes on an especially hectic morning. In that short amount of time my toddler managed to break into the bathroom, where I found him dipping his paci in and out of the toilet while holding a dead bug in his other hand. (This actually happened one morning—judge me, I dare you.)

I could've cried that day, but I didn't, actually. I laughed, because I had to in order to *keep* from crying. And even then— I was still enough. And so are you. You're killing the game because you're here, you're showing up, and you're trying. You're enough for your kids. Even on your worst day. There are no perfect kids.

And there's no perfect mom. Perfection may be something that culture calls us to, but it's not something Jesus ever calls us to.

"For by one sacrifice he has made perfect forever those who are being made holy" (Hebrews 10:14 NIV).

We don't have to strive for perfection, because Jesus hasn't called us to be perfect. He has already covered us with a perfect love. Meditate on that today—even if you only have five minutes between laundry loads, work Zooms, or errand stops. Just close your eyes and think about Jesus' perfect love for us. How His thoughts for you outnumber the grains of sand. You are already *so loved*. Isn't that enough to get you through the day?

> Perfection may be something that culture calls us to, but it's not something Jesus ever calls us to.

In my journey to healing, I had to begin believing that God's grace was bigger than my regret. That maybe, just maybe, if I placed a little bit of the weight of my life, my healing on Him, that He would meet me there. That He would come running and meet me there.

And just like every other area of our lives that needs healing, we can't—and don't have to—do it alone. Find other moms you trust. Meet with them. Yeah, I get it. Who has the time? But make the time. Even if it's a park date with the kids, at least you can grab some bench time while you are making sure your kid doesn't break his leg on the slide.

Talk to your husband about how important other mom

friendships and face time are for you. That way, you can plan ahead for that one night a week when you can meet with that friend—or friends—to catch up, swap "bad mom" stories, and laugh. And, hopefully, give each other permission to be human. To be the imperfect but completely-loved-by-God mom that He created you to be.

Chapter 23

HALFWAY SUCKS

Anybody else totally obsessed with holidays? It's like a scheduled new experience every year—it's an Enneagram seven's total dream.

I moved to Nashville to start the girl group in the month of August. One of the girls was from the area, so she already knew a lot of people and had a community of friends. The rest of us had moved from different states and knew no one but each other. So when the Nashville native suggested we host a Halloween party at our house, she gave us an incentive: "I'll invite all my friends." We were all probably *too* eager to meet new people, so we were totally in.

We threw the party a week before Halloween, because our label made us do this terrible Christian boat cruise on the actual day. The point of the entire trip was to build industry relationships and network, but we all ended up almost getting kicked off the boat because we were wearing bikinis and being too loud.

No, you read that correctly.

Anyway, so we threw this huge Halloween party and tons of people showed up.

So obviously we dressed as the Spice Girls because—five girls, pop group—it just made sense. I was Ginger Spice—you know, with the red hair. I went *all out*. No detail went un-thought-through. It was probably my best costume ever, which explains why my husband fell in love with me that night.

I had one contact in Nashville before I moved there, and I invited him to come hang out as friends. He asked me if he could bring some buddies with him—some guys from a Christian recording group called Anthem Lights. I said, "The more, the merrier." Which was really more like, "The more, the less likely I am to have to hold a conversation with my bandmates, who hate me."

Anthem Lights walked in and I noticed my now husband Caleb right away. Only...I wasn't interested. I had always dated athletes—like tall, big dudes. Caleb is not much taller than I am, and he struck me as one of those artsy boy band types. (You know, someone with an actual brain, a sensitive side, and capacity for independent thought. *The horror.*)

The party was actually one of my more enjoyable experiences with the girls' group—we had fun. And I would find out later that Caleb had fun, too. In fact, he'd noticed me. His friends asked him, "So, you got your eye on anyone from the party?" And he was like, "The redhead. For sure, the redhead."

They started teasing him or whatever, and Caleb said, "You know what? I think I may actually marry that girl." As for me, I was still seeing Jeremy the Grade-A Jerk at the time, and hadn't been attracted to Caleb at first because he just wasn't my typical type.

Also, I was not in a good place. It wasn't many nights later that I wanted to drive myself off that infamous rain-soaked bridge. I wouldn't have known where to find something that was good for me if someone had drawn out a map and explained the route. *(So…at the next drunken stupor, take a right toward wholeness. When you reach it, there's a pothole of dark depression there, so veer right toward freedom.)*

I was a couple of weeks into counseling when Caleb reached out. We had been low-key flirting over Twitter (JTGAJ was out like the garbage that he was), but I still had no business toying with the idea of dating. We kept up the social media dialogue for a while, but I was terrified to take it anywhere else.

After getting to know Caleb a little better, I was like, *I think he might actually be good to me. And I can't accept it. I'm not worthy. I'll kill it. I will sabotage this before it's ever a thing. That's what I do. And that's the only thing that's safe to me anymore.*

At that point, I was of the mindset that I'd rather have been used than loved, because I felt completely unlovable. I couldn't be with a guy like Caleb. He was actually *sweet*. He was actually *kind*. He was actually *good*.

Nope, I thought. *Go find yourself a kindergarten teacher named Rebecca who loves Jesus and can give you an easy, peaceful life.*

I was like, *If this guy falls in love with me, I'm going to break his heart. I'd rather someone just be mean to me, because that's what I deserve.*

I went back home for my birthday, which is a few days after

Christmas. And I'll never forget it, but Caleb called me on the actual day to wish me a happy birthday.

He called me. Like, with an actual phone using his actual voice. And he formally asked me on a date. In my whole life, I'd never had a guy do that. I was so taken aback that I agreed before I could talk myself out of it.

When I got back to Nashville, Caleb came and picked me up. He had flowers. He opened the car door for me. He'd planned the entire evening. Caleb had a friend who was a ballroom dance teacher, and he knew how obsessed I was with all things Disney, so we learned the bolero to the song "A Whole New World." At the time, our manager had forbidden us to drink because we all basically acted like lunatics when alcohol was in the equation. Caleb had virgin mimosas waiting for us at the dance studio—he'd thought of everything. Every little detail.

After our dance lesson, we went and had Italian food. Which, honestly, would have been enough on its own, because that's how much I love pasta. Then, we went back to his house, where he'd bought *Aladdin* on DVD and had chocolate waiting for me. He didn't kiss me that night. But he asked if he could hold my hand, which is just about the most precious thing ever.

Never, besides my own father, had I ever been treated with such respect. With such *honor*.

My first thought the next morning was, *Okay. What's wrong with this guy? This is too good to be true. There has to be something the matter with him. Like, he can't really be this nice. He's probably an ax murderer. He has to be a serial killer or something, right?*

Later, I told Rob about the date and about Caleb. It wasn't

two months earlier that I had been considering ending my life, and Rob said, "Kelsey, you can't seriously be entertaining the idea of a relationship right now."

"Oh, no," I told him. "I don't want a relationship with him. I don't deserve him. I'll break him."

"No, no, no. That's not what I'm saying," Rob said. "What I'm saying is you're not ready. You haven't even told your parents what happened with Chris yet. You haven't even begun to find healing. If you don't figure out your mess now, you're just going to drag it into your next relationship. You are not ready, and you have to tell this guy that today."

But when you tell a seven they can't do something, it just makes them want to do it more. Not only that, but Caleb was the *one* good thing in my life. The one place that I felt like maybe I could be normal again. I wrestled with the decision, but eventually agreed with Rob. Honestly, I was too tired to argue with him about it. And deep down, I knew he was right.

"Just tell him you need to push pause," Rob said. "Tell him that you're not sure how long it'll be, but that you have some work to do on yourself before you can be in a healthy relationship. And if he's as great as you say he is, he'll understand. And it'll all work out when you're ready for it."

I called Caleb and pulled the plug on the entire relationship. I was very vague. I told him I'd been through some trauma and that I was working on it for the very first time. I told him that I'd let him know when that changed.

And look, I know that it sounded like a total cop-out when I said, "It's not you; it's me," but it was the truth. Later on, he would tell me that his friends gave him the hardest time. Like,

"Dude, she's just not that into you. No one actually says, 'It's not you; it's me.' You need to let that girl go. You need to move on."

But I felt terrible about it. Actually, I was devastated. This guy had just pulled out all the stops to take me on the single most romantic, most thoughtful date of my entire life. He was the first gentleman I had ever met. I had spent so much time saying yes to the wrong things, and there I was, saying no to the right thing. It felt counterintuitive. More than that, it felt risky. I didn't want to lose that good thing.

But Rob was right. I just wasn't ready. I knew that saying yes to the right thing at the wrong time still doesn't make that thing right. It makes a right thing wrong. It was like what I talked about earlier—we hate halfway. (Well, I sure do.) Being told "Let's just wait and see." And for me, Miss Enneagram Seven, clicking pause just wasn't how I rolled. But I did it. And it was hard.

"I need you to stop texting me, to stop calling me for the foreseeable future," I told him. "And when I'm in a better spot, when I've healed a little, I'll call you. And if you're still open, I would like to see you again."

As horrible as it was, pressing pause with Caleb was the right move. As much as I wanted his love, deep down I felt like I was unworthy of it. I had no idea what I thought about God anymore. I still hadn't really begun to confront

I knew that saying yes to the right thing at the wrong time still doesn't make that thing right.

the trauma of my relationship with Chris. I was a mess—the stench of my past still following me around like cheap-smelling perfume.

And because I was somewhere halfway in my treatment and recovery, if I had moved ahead with Caleb, I think I would have been moving ahead of what God wanted. Does that make sense? It's kind of like the story we all heard as kids in Sunday school (or whatever your church called it) about the Israelites in the wilderness. Some of them looked back toward captivity in Egypt and yearned for it. (Crazy, right? They had been *slaves*.) Well, part of myself—the part that was driven by fear—wanted to just stay where I was.

Halfway. That image just kind of lies there, doesn't it? That's not what we want! We want the fresh beginning or the brilliant ending. But halfway? Pfft. Halfway sucks. The unfinished business. The half-read book or interrupted Netflix movie. Problem is, God's sense of "finished" is often very different from our own.

Cruel taskmaster? Cosmic jokester? Nah. Stopping halfway across the wilderness isn't His style. When we do try to stop halfway through our [fill in the terrible experience here: addiction recovery; path back from divorce; grieving period after a spouse has been unfaithful], God nudges us on. He makes it *really* hard for us to feel comfortable living in the wilderness.

But going forward can be terrifying. For me, I thought, *What if I just can't pull it off?* As in, get healthy and become a "whole" person (whatever that looks like). Going back to captivity (for me, "Egypt" looked like drinking, numbing myself, staying stuck in shame) would have been easy. But I think it would have cost me a lot—maybe everything. Would I even still be alive? It most definitely would have cost me my relationship with the man I would eventually marry.

And do you know what Caleb did when I said I needed a break? He respected my wishes. He did what I asked. He didn't call me. He didn't text me.

And I was *furious*. And yes, I am laughing!

But see…I knew deep down that *that* was the kind of person God had for me. Not just another *guy* (there are lots of JTGAJ-type guys out there), but a *man*. A man who could see me and respect me, even if he didn't fully understand.

"This is your fault," I told Rob one day. "He's gone. I haven't heard a word from him. He's probably found another girl and he's moved on. He was a *good* thing. He was a *good* thing, and I let him slip right through my fingertips, and I will probably never get him back again."

In his quiet, unaffected way Rob just nodded. "I hear you, Kelsey. I hear you. You know, I'm sorry that you feel like that. I'm sorry you're feeling hurt. But I give you my word, you're going to thank me for this someday."

Rob knew what I didn't yet—that sometimes, in order to get to our good thing, we have to risk losing it. Thankfully for me, it didn't take forty years of wandering around the desert.

Time passed, and Rob and I did the hard work of unpacking my relationship with Chris. With every session of therapy, every word I confessed, every step I took back toward God, I felt lighter. It was like each and every secret, lie, and bad decision I'd made was a brick. And I'd picked up those bricks along the way and put them in a bag and slung them over my shoulder. My body ached from the weight of them.

Then, while working with Rob, the unloading of those bricks took time. It took honesty. But one day, I looked at my life and was shocked—my bag of bricks was almost empty. And with it? I had begun to build something new. A foundation that resembled truth and stability.

A few months later, with Rob's blessing, I reached out to Caleb. "Would you be willing to reconnect? I'd like to talk."

He agreed, and I went to his place and sat on his couch. I told him as much of the truth as I appropriately could. I did. I just led with it. Something inside of me told me that Caleb was important. That he needed more than just "I'm better now. Yay! Let's make out." Caleb deserved answers.

I was crying, and I told him, "For the first time, I've come to realize that what I experienced a year and a half ago was a really abusive relationship. It was sexually abusive. And I have a lot of baggage, Caleb. I could open up an Amazon distribution center with it. But I want you to know that going into this, and I want to give you a fair opportunity to walk away if that's what you want to do. And I would totally understand—I'm a lot to take on. I'm still working through a lot, but if you're still in, I'd like to give us a try."

Looking back, I could almost laugh. I went from hiding the truth to vomiting (sorry to use *that* word) it all over poor Caleb. I said it almost like a dare. Almost like, *See? You don't want me. See? You're just going to leave. See? You should have never wasted your feelings, your emotions on me.*

But I meant what I said. I can't undo my past. None of us

can. But we can learn from it. We can grow from it. We can become better because of it. Our past becomes most useful when it *informs* our future—not when it defines it.

Caleb's response was beautiful. He's so tender. So sensitive. He had tears in his eyes. He said, "I'm so sorry, Kelsey. I'm so sorry that happened to you."

I would have married him right then and there.

He went on, "I don't need to know the details right now. Just know that this breaks my heart for you. No one should go through that. And just so you know, I'm not scared. This doesn't scare me. Your past doesn't scare me. It only makes me care about you more."

How on earth was this possible?

You mean, when the Bible says "And the truth will set you free" (John 8:32), it actually means that the truth sets us free? You mean, when God tells us that it pleases Him for us to tell the truth (see Proverbs 12:22), we actually see the results of His joy, of His pride, in our own lives?

I didn't believe it. I was still afraid. I would tell myself, *Caleb doesn't really know what happened. He doesn't know what he's saying. He doesn't know what he's agreeing to. He doesn't know how bad I really am. Once he finds out everything, he'll bolt.*

The thing about our freedom in Jesus is that we have to protect it. We have to fight for it, sometimes. Because as soon as we gain ground, fear will try to drag us back. Fear will tell us all kinds of twisted lies to steal as much of our joy as it can. Fear will try, but fear doesn't have to—and shouldn't—win.

We had been dating a few weeks when I sat Caleb down to tell him the *whole* truth. I needed him to know. I needed to invite him in a little further. I needed to look fear in the eye and tell it to put up or shut up.

So I told him. I left out no detail. And we both just sat across from each other and we both cried. I'll never forget what Caleb said.

"I love you, Kelsey. I knew I loved you before this conversation. But if it's possible, I love you even more, now. You've been through so much. But you're so strong. Any man would be lucky to have you on his arm."

Writing that now makes me cry. So many times in our relationship, Caleb has been an example of God's love for me. Unconditional. Overwhelming. Nonsensical, at times. If we had any idea how much God loves us, we would absolutely fall to our knees in awe and wonder.

When I let go of my expectations that Caleb would reject me, when I stopped being "good" and started being real, I gave him a chance to love me like God does. With no caveats or conditions. I gave him a chance to know me—to see me. And there's no greater feeling on this side of heaven than being fully known and fully loved by another human being.

And by God.

Chapter 24

PRAYING HEAVEN DOWN

Caleb and I got married in 2014 and knew we wanted to start a family sooner rather than later, but our goal was to be married for a year first. We made it to that goal and then started trying for kid number one. We were so excited to add to the love we shared together; though imperfect, we'd found our corner in the universe together and wanted to share it with our baby.

I loved being pregnant with my first child. I loved watching my belly grow and feeling every kick, wiggle, and movement. It was amazing. Today it reminds me of that little girl Kels with her Bitty Baby doll. It was like God poured mamahood into my genetic code. I felt like I was born to be a mom.

Well, the pregnancy journey was amazing until the last two months, when Emmett decided to practice his kickboxing skills against my rib cage.

About twenty-three weeks into my pregnancy, Caleb and I

transferred our prenatal care from the hospital to a birthing center here in Nashville that provides a holistic approach to birth and babies. We were able to do all of our appointments there in these posh, cozy birthing suites—each equipped with queen-size beds, birthing tubs, and other natural pain-management methods.

In my naïveté, I had decided about halfway through my pregnancy that the hospital setting/doctors' office environment wasn't for me. I didn't like the idea of how sterile it felt, the fact that hospitals can seem like businesses just trying to turn beds over, and how often women seem rushed through their labor and delivery, which can ultimately lead to unnecessary caesarians.

I thought I wanted to feel the natural pains of labor while bringing Emmett into the world. I wanted to feel like I was in control of my labor. And I trusted that my body was designed to do this.

I had a plan, y'all. Which is basically the cardinal rule of parenting—do not make plans for how your kid will do anything, including how they'll be born.

Because, oh, how different things turned out to be.

My body never went into labor on its own. I tried *all* the natural things in the book to try and bribed my body to do what I thought it could on its own. But Emmett was comfy cozy in his mama's belly and was like, "Nah, I'll just stay in here."

When I reached forty-one weeks, my midwife required me to get an ultrasound, because I was late enough that there were concerns of decreasing amniotic fluid levels, which could lead to potential dangers for the baby. So, I went in at the beginning of that week for an ultrasound to check on little E. It turns out, he wasn't so little. The tech informed me that Emmett was measuring to be about nine pounds. Which, if you know what Caleb and I look like, you'll understand why this sounded so ridiculous to us. (I'm laughing as I even type this.) We are two of the smallest people in the world, and yet somehow, this tech was telling us we were going to have a *huge* baby.

Naturally, I immediately panicked and started to second-guess everything I had planned for my labor and delivery. I began doubting my body's ability to birth a nine-pound baby without the help of drugs. All my plans. All my dreams. All my expectations were crushed under the weight of my new reality.

I burst into tears on the ultrasound table. But Caleb assured me that I was absolutely capable. That I was strong, and that I needed to trust the people taking care of me to help me bring my baby into the world the way I wanted to and had planned.

We followed up with my midwife that day, who told me that ultrasound techs were almost always off on their predictions of a baby's weight and size, and that I didn't need to worry about that. She did, however, tell me that if at any point I wanted to forgo the birthing center option and choose a hospital induction instead, that I absolutely could and they would support that.

I decided to give it a few more days to see if Emmett would come on his own. He didn't. Apparently, my steady diet of tacos and chips and salsa made for quite the luxurious baby palace.

After careful consideration, prayer, another phone call to my midwife, and the support of our family, Caleb and I felt it was best to abandon our birth plan at the birthing center and schedule an induction for Wednesday, November 30, 2017, at 8:00 p.m. at Vanderbilt Medical Center.

I was eleven days late at that point, with no signs of labor whatsoever.

I was heartbroken to go another route with my birth plan that I had so carefully written and prayed over for so many months. In a way, I already felt like such a failure to my son for "giving in" and opting for drugs that would force my body to go into labor. At the time, my plan was so important; my plan was all that mattered. Why wasn't God on the same plan as I was?

(For anyone thinking I sound like a pretentious know-it-all, please be advised that I was a first-time mother who just wanted what I felt was best for my baby.)

However, now, three babies later, I welcome modern medicine and anything that keeps me from feeling like my body is being snapped in two. I am not critiquing any particular birthing method—natural, medicinal, or otherwise. It's an individual decision, and different for everyone.

I wrestled the entire two-day waiting period, begging God to allow my body to go into labor on its own, before my scheduled induction. Nope. Wasn't going to happen. Needless to say, Wednesday was a crazy day of cleaning the house (a desperate attempt to distract from my nervousness about what was coming that night), last-minute errands, and nursery tweaks to make sure everything was perfect when we would come home with our little one just a couple of days later.

On the way to the hospital I turned to Caleb. "I'm excited but I'm also sad, babe," I said. "This just isn't what I expected."

He held my hand and said all the right things, but we were both bummed (and scared).

We checked into the hospital that night and were taken to

our birthing room. I went into this process still wanting to stick as closely to my original plan as possible, even though the environment was going to be different. I wanted to labor naturally as long as I could and experience everything that comes with it.

Such a seven. Even in childbearing, I didn't want to miss out on an experience.

They started my IV, and not long after that, I was given a pill that was supposed to begin "ripening my cervix." Yup. The ole cervix—just like a piece of fruit.

In other words, the pill would thrust my body into labor.

I explained to the midwife there that I wanted to labor naturally as long as I could. Bless her heart, she was so careful with her words. She said, "Kelsey, I respect your decision on that. And we can do that as long as you want. But I just want you to know that induced labors are very different from natural labors when the body does this on its own. Induced contractions are much more difficult to withstand because they are not the body's natural way of getting the baby out."

"I'll be fine," I said, still clinging to my plan, clinging to my expectations.

"Okay," she said. Then, as her final, gentle warning, "You may experience fast and furious contractions that don't give way to breaks in between. I can count on *one* finger"—she said *finger* and not *hand*—"the number of women who have been induced and been able to give birth naturally. It's just very hard."

"I'll be fine," I repeated.

"Okay. You are welcome to try as long as you'd like. And if you change your mind, an epidural is right around the corner and there's no shame in that."

But then I won't get my way, Nurse Nancy.

I forged ahead. About forty-five minutes later, I experienced my first contraction. And no, it wasn't "like bad gas." It was like getting-punched-in-the-groin bad.

"They're coming," I told Caleb. "And they're coming fast."

Nurse Nancy was right. The contractions were coming faster than I could breathe. I would get ten, maybe fifteen seconds between each one. I was barely surviving one contraction before the next one started.

They seemed to get stronger and stronger, and just when I thought they couldn't get any worse, they did.

And, man, if my stubbornness were ever evident, it was that day. I labored like this for over three hours.

We were deep into the night by then, and I was in excruciating pain. The midwife came in to check me to see how much progress I had made after those grueling hours of contractions.

Because surely, they wouldn't be for nothing. Surely, I'd be close to pushing by that point. She checked my cervix and gave me the news—I was at two centimeters. The exact number I came into the hospital at.

Eight more centimeters? I had to endure what I had just endured times *four*?

"Your body simply isn't responding to the contractions, Kelsey," she told me. "I'm sorry."

I instantly burst into tears.

I'm never enough, my old wounds told me. *Never enough.*

I knew it was going to be a really long night. I also knew that I couldn't make it without the help of some medication.

Minutes later, the anesthesiologist came into the room, and Caleb stayed with me while they administered the spinal needle for an epidural. While I was sitting there having this done, my water broke on the table. Of course. And immediately following that, another massive contraction. But I had to hold ever-so-still while they put the needle in that would finally bring some relief to the last few hours I'd spent laboring.

After the epidural, my labor became tolerable. It definitely wasn't pain-canceling, but it made my contractions less obvious to me, and much more bearable.

For the next twelve hours or so, I continued to labor with Caleb and my mom at my side.

I was so tired. Worn-out. Still progressing so slowly. Finally, the next day and after about twenty-one hours of labor, my midwife came to check my cervix.

"I have wonderful news," she told me. "It's time to start pushing."

"Actually," I said, "I can't push today." I was only half-conscious at that point, exhausted and defeated. "Let's do tomorrow instead."

I am being dead serious—that seemed like the most logical course of action to me at the time.

"I just need to sleep."

Isn't it funny what your mind thinks is rational after no sleep and hours of labor?

"Um, Kelsey," she said. "That's not how this works."

So I mustered up some adrenaline and motivation, because I knew that I was finally about to meet my baby.

The first hour of pushing was exhilarating. I felt like I was so close to meeting him—our son. Our baby. But then I grew tired again. In fact, I would push for thirty seconds, and then fall asleep for thirty seconds until it was time to push again. I was crying, I was frustrated, and I was beyond exhausted.

I had been in labor for twenty-four hours and I sensed that the medical staff was getting a little concerned. "Focus, Kelsey. Focus," my midwife would say. "Push."

But with each contraction, Emmett's heart rate was dropping. I *needed* to get this baby out.

Finally, Jenna, one of our midwives, got the attention of everyone in the room—a room that had become very full of friends and family, by that point. And this was another detail I would *never* have planned, but one that I'm deeply thankful for in hindsight (because each of them played a vital role, as you'll see in a minute).

"We need to pray," she said bluntly. "We need to pray that baby Emmett makes his way into this world quickly."

My dad led the room in prayer. Minutes later, with the entire room cheering me on, Emmett Rhodes was laid on my chest. The entire group erupted into cheers and sobs—relief, sweet relief.

Which lasted all of about ten seconds.

I instantly knew something was very wrong. My son started to turn blue in my arms. The midwives furiously rubbed and prodded Emmett to try to initiate that first sound every mother longs to hear when their baby enters the world—his cry. But it was silent. Dead silent.

"Why isn't he crying?" I asked. "Why isn't he crying yet?"

"He will," a midwife told me. "Everything's okay."

But their actions didn't line up with their words. They quickly pulled Caleb over to cut the cord (which I originally wanted to be delayed for the baby's benefit), but they informed me it needed to be done, and done quickly.

I realized then that Emmett wasn't crying because he wasn't breathing.

I blinked and everything became a blur.

The door flew open and in ran nine NICU doctors and nurses. They were working on my baby—doing something to him that I couldn't see. I lay helplessly on the hospital bed, bloody, confused, horrified.

My bed split the room in two—my friends and family on the left, the medical team and Emmett on the right.

I started to scream. Irrational, psychotic screaming.

"*What is going on?!* Somebody tell me. Please. What's happening with my baby?"

Caleb draped himself over me to try to keep my thrashing body from flying off the table as I wailed uncontrollably. He tried to yell over my screams into my ear—prayers for our baby, who wasn't breathing, encouragement that he would be okay. Caleb told me later he had no idea what was going to happen. And that, like me, he worried we'd leave the hospital empty-handed in every way.

In the sheer panic and chaos that ensued for the next few minutes as the NICU team rushed to save my baby boy, there was a moment in time I will never forget—another movie moment.

I remember feeling trapped between two worlds almost. I

looked to my left. There was my village: my mom; Tyler; my other brother, Chad, and his wife; and one of my best friends. They were all on their knees on the hospital floor, praying, begging God to let Emmett breathe. Caleb and my dad stood by my head, praying loudly, sobbing.

Me? I just screamed.

I looked to my right.

Blue lab coats everywhere. They were talking to one another urgently. I have no idea how they could hear anything over the cacophony of grief coming from the left side of the room. All I knew was no one was turning around to tell this terrified mama that her son was going to be okay. Because they couldn't make that promise to me in that moment.

I looked left again and through my screams, I heard someone yell the name of Jesus.

Then I heard Caleb's voice pierce through all the others and utter, "Jesus."

And before I knew it, I was screaming out the only thing I had left. *"Jesus!"*

It still feels like we prayed heaven down into that room in those moments.

That first, feeble cry. It cut through the room like a mighty sword and everyone grew quiet.

"He's breathing," a doctor yelled over his shoulder. "We're still helping him, but he's breathing."

Minutes later, still very pale, very lethargic, but undeniably alive, I got to hold my baby boy, wrapped in a blanket and wide-eyed. He had fought his way back into my arms, and I was bowled over with gratitude and relief.

Why do I tell you this story? Why did I choose to end my entire book with *this* story? Well, for one, who doesn't love a good, traumatic birth story? Am I right? If you've never had a baby, you're probably scarred for life. Don't worry—my other two deliveries were delightfully boring. I chose to tell you this story because, in our lives, the expectations we'll have to work the hardest to overcome will be *our own*.

I think so much of my story would have been different had I just given myself a freaking break—had I eased my need to control just a little. I had very different expectations for how we would meet Emmett, but in the end, God had another plan. God used that situation to teach Caleb and me so much about parenting. About how precious life is and how powerful our God is.

We have to let go over and over and over again. It hurts, but it's worth it.

And it really never stops—that low-key hum of the world that wants to turn us toward doing instead of being. Comparing instead of accepting. Judging instead of loving.

Freedom takes vigilance—it takes work. Sound contradictory? It's not. We have to remain on our guard, attentive to the voices in our head. Have you ever considered the fact that most of the thoughts rolling around in our head are not life-giving? But the more we allow God in—surrender our thought life to Him—the more peace we find.

We have to let go of our expectations every single day. Expectations from others, from our culture, and even from ourselves. But every time we lean away from what we're expected to be and into who we already are as God's loved and adored children, we experience freedom. We live into ourselves and find confidence there.

We can get beyond it—that old life of striving, working, and clawing for acceptance. It really is possible to get over it.

Because we are enough

Already.

EPILOGUE

There was a time in my life when I swore I would never tell this story. When I was sure that shame would always own me.

Not long after I'd told my parents about what happened with Chris, I remember telling my mom I would never get married. That I would never allow myself to fall in love again because it would only lead to hurt.

She paused, then looked at me and calmly but confidently said, "Baby, borrow my faith. You'll love again. And you'll *be* loved again. And someday, you'll have the opportunity to tell this story and share it with the world. Can you imagine how many girls and women might be set free someday because of your bravery? Because of your vulnerability to talk about it?"

To be honest, on that day, I couldn't imagine it. I couldn't fathom telling even my best friend at the time, let alone the rest of the world. But here I am, sharing it with you. Putting it into the world in hopes that someone—anyone—might find the courage to break free of a life of unhealthy and unrealistic expectations. My mom was right that day. And I'm so glad she was.

My hope is that this book breathes life into dry bones. Sheds light into the souls of the ones living in darkness. And helps remind you over and over of a divine love that's pursuing you with reckless abandon at every moment. Because you, my friend, are so utterly and infinitely loved.

A few years back, I wrote a blog post about my relationship with Chris and the sexual and emotional abuse I endured while with him. I purposefully didn't use his name and didn't include any distinguishing characteristics about the situation. The truth is, I don't want to hurt him. Not because he doesn't deserve it, but because I'm not a total monster and the point of sharing my story was never to ruin someone else's life. And I have to believe he has changed and is a better man. He apologized to me. I've forgiven him (though as I have said, at times the bitterness and hatred rears its head). And I'd like to hope that the Chris I knew then doesn't exist anymore.

A couple of days after I posted, I received a message on Facebook. Here's what it said:

Hello, Kelsey. You don't know me, and to be honest, I don't really know you. Because the only things I have heard about you came from the person you most recently shared about—Chris. I dated Chris for two years many, many, many years ago. Since then, I've been married and my husband and I have kids. My husband is the only person I've ever told the truth to—the truth about my past with Chris. To this day, I am still haunted by dreams and nightmares and memories. There have been times when I've let what Chris did to me control my life. It's affected my marriage—especially our sexual connection. A friend we have in common shared your blog with me and I bawled my eyes out the whole way through. I am so very sorry for everything that happened to you. It happened to me, too. I want you to know that reading your words has encouraged me to get the help that I've been needing to get for the last ten years. Thank you for being so brave and obedient.

Reading her message unleashed a river of tears. I wasn't the only one. She'd dated Chris *before* me. Were there others who dated him after me that were also traumatized?

What if I had stood up sooner? What if I had been braver, more honest, more like *Who gives a crap about people's expectations?*

I believe I processed my trauma in God's perfect timing, so I won't what-if myself into an oblivion over this, but instead, move forward with it as an invaluable lesson.

We're all messed up. That's why God sent us Jesus—so that we could come home to Him. And you may have to come home more than once. I have. But I believe that if we can all learn to just be real—to just own our mess instead of covering it up and wasting precious moments of our lives, we can all begin to heal.

I'm over it.

I'm over worrying about what other people think.

I'm over worrying about what a culture expects from me.

I'm over worrying about the wrong things.

And I hope, after reading my story, you'll be over it, too.

ACKNOWLEDGMENTS

Thank you first and foremost to Jesus. For grace and love I'll never be able to wrap my mind around. For giving me an opportunity to share my honest story with the world. My hope is that people read this and realize how recklessly pursued they are by You because of it.

Thank you to my husband, my rock, my biggest support and cheerleader—Caleb, you went to heights and depths that no one else has, to show me how much you love me—every version of me. You are the reason I took a chance on love again, and I'm infinitely grateful that I did. We've built a beautifully messy life together, and I can't imagine doing it with anyone else. Thank you for seeing light in me when it isn't even there. You're my number one.

Thank you to my family. My mama and daddy—you believed in me and abandoned a comfortable life you knew and loved to pursue a relationship with me when I was still living in darkness. I am who I am in part because of you. Tyler—you very literally picked me up off the floor when I couldn't stand and carried me through the darkest season of my life. You saved me. Because of that, our souls are bound in a way I don't share with another person. Chad, your transparency and your dreamer mentality have inspired me more times than I can count. And to

Sarah Mae—for loving my kids as your own and for freeing up time for me to invest in getting this story written. I couldn't have done it without your dedication to our family.

To Grammy—you always have been (and still are) my biggest fan on the planet. I love you so very much.

And to Lys—my best friend. You're the closest thing I've ever had to a sister. Some people spend a lifetime searching for a friend like you—one who loves and supports without question or hesitation. And you've done that and more for me for almost two decades now. (Why are we so old?) I also wouldn't survive motherhood without you. Miles might separate us, but they sure as hell can't keep us apart. I adore you.

To Renee—you came into my life at such a pivotal time, shortly after I became a mama for the first time. You've spoken truth and calm encouragement into me and have helped me step into myself with grace and acceptance so many times. Thank you for championing me in all of my crazy life endeavors.

To Esther—thank you for that call we had while I paced in a Starbucks parking lot two years ago when I told you my story for the first time. Thank you for immediately taking a chance on me and never looking back. Your belief in me along the way has never wavered.

To Bryan Ward—this wouldn't have happened without you, and I'm forever grateful.

To Josh and Mark (and the rest of my amazing team at Prodigy)—you've taken this ball and carried it down the court on many days when I felt like I couldn't. You've fielded my tearful phone calls on bad days and talked me down when I needed it. You've spearheaded so much of this process, and you've stood in my corner every step of the way. Your vision, follow-through, and support of me have taken this to places I never dreamed.

To Holly and Kyle—you very literally helped me put my story and heart on paper. You both held my heart along the way, encouraging me and helping me stay true to myself and be brave in it. Your work and expertise on this project made it possible.

To Hachette and my incredible team there—thank you for the day we sat around that big round table and for seeing potential in me. Thank you for accepting me with open arms and for letting me write this book as rawly and honestly as I hoped someone would someday.

And last but never least—to my babies. Emmett, Beckett, and Collins, I hope you read this book someday and are proud. I've been places I never wish for you to experience, but if you do—I want you to know that no valley is too dark to climb out of. And nothing you could ever do or become will change my love for you. I am so proud and honored simply because you're mine. You three are my very heart walking around outside my body. You're the reason for everything. You're my why. Now and always. You've already taught me so much more about life and love than anyone. I love you so infinitely.

And to you reading this—thank you for going on this journey with me. For giving me a safe space to be myself and share my story with you.

NOTES

1. "Finding Strength in the Midst of Disappointment (Part 1 of 2)," Focus on the Family Broadcast, January 14, 2020, https://www.focusonthefamily.com/episodes/broadcast/finding-strength-in-the-midst-of-disappointment-part-1-of-2.

2. Michael Slepian, "Why the Secrets You Keep Are Hurting You," *Scientific American*, February 5, 2019, https://www.scientificamerican.com/article/why-the-secrets-you-keep-are-hurting-you.

3. Jeremy Myers, "Grace Is Absolutely Free! No, Really!" Redeeming God (blog), undated, https://redeeminggod.com/grace-absolutely-free.

4. "Porn Survey," available through Proven Men Ministries, https://www.provenmen.org/2014PornSurvey.

5. "Pornography Statistics," Covenant Eyes, https://www.covenanteyes.com/pornstats.

6. "The Porn Phenomenon," Barna.com, 2016, https://www.barna.com/the-porn-phenomenon.

7. Dolores Sanchez, "Mother Teresa, a Suffering and Depressed Saint," Mental Health Justice Blog, March 16, 2016, http://www.mentalhealthjustice.net/blog/2016/3/14/53sdjv7bzb4g3cdwqw2b97mwi2ppls.

8. "Words Everyone Seems to Hate," Word Counter, February 3, 2017, https://wordcounter.net/blog/2017/02/03/102922_words-people-hate.html.

ABOUT THE AUTHOR

Kelsey Grimm is known by most as a singer/artist alongside her husband, Caleb, in their duo, Caleb+Kelsey. She also considers herself a stay-at-home mom, with the majority of her time spent raising their three beautiful babies in Nashville, TN. Kelsey is an enthusiastic, vibrant adrenaline junkie who craves deep, meaningful relationships, below-the-surface conversation, and an occasional good glass of wine. She's passionate about pursuing a life that's honest and bold—learning to see herself through the eyes of the Divine, while encouraging others to do the same.